Italian Menus

Great Meals in Minutes was created by Rebus Inc., and
published by Time-Life Books.

This edition published 1994 by Bloomsbury Books, an
imprint of The Godfrey Cave Group, 42 Bloomsbury Street,
London, WC1B 3QJ.

© 1994 Time-Life Books BV.

ISBN 1 85471 571 2

Printed and bound in Great Britain.

Italian Menus

Silvana La Rocca

Menu 1
Stuffed Porcini Mushrooms — 8
Chicken with Peppers
Radicchio and Mozzarella Salad

Menu 2
Fillets of Sole Signora Concetta — 10
Baked Onions
Fresh Tomato Salad

Menu 3
Spicy Lamb Chops — 12
Hunter-style Potatoes
Green Beans with Mint

Felice and Lidia Bastianich

Menu 1
Scampi with Quick Risotto — 16
Asparagus Gratinati

Menu 2
Quail with Polenta — 18
Green Bean, Red Onion, and Bacon Salad

Menu 3
Chicken Felice — 21
Swiss Chard and Potatoes

Lynne Kasper

Menu 1
Escarole, Onion, and Coppa Salad — 24
Peasant-style Risotto

Menu 2
Renaissance Almond Broth — 26
Sweet and Savoury Grilled Lamb
Herb-Roasted Potatoes

Menu 3
Prosciutto and Mostarda di Cremona — 29
Minestrone with Chickpeas

Susan DeRege

Menu 1
Piedmontese Pork Medallions — 34
Straw and Hay Pasta with Butter Sauce
Carrots with Kirsch

Menu 2
Chicken Breasts Milanese — 36
Risotto with Porcini Mushrooms
Endive salad with Green Herb Sauce

Menu 3
Cream of Artichoke Soup — 39
Veal Scallopini Cavour
Peperonata

Nancy Verde Barr

Menu 1
Braised Duck with Black Olives — 44
Penne with Mushroom Sauce

Menu 2
Piquant Chicken — 46
Baked Stuffed Tomatoes

Menu 3
Courgette Soup — 49
Lamb Catanzaro-style
Broccoli Rabe

Robert Pucci

Menu 1
Braised Beef Tenderloin in Wine Sauce — 54
Potatoes Parmigiana
Sautéed Vegetables

Menu 2
Linguine with Clam Sauce — 56
Fillets of Flounder Sorrento
Sautéed Spinach with Pine Nuts and Raisins

Menu 3
Angel Hair Pasta with Onions and Pepper Strips — 58
Veal Scallopini Marsala
Warm Vegetable Salad

Bloomsbury Books
London

Silvana La Rocca

Menu 1
(*right*)
Stuffed Porcini Mushrooms
Chicken with Peppers
Radicchio and Mozzarella Salad

Born into an Italian family that subscribes to the ancient saying *la civiltà sta nel piatto* (civilization can be found on a plate), Silvana La Rocca was exposed to good cooking and fine dining at an early age. Her maternal grandmother taught her how to make fresh pasta; her mother introduced her to the vast diversity of Italian cooking; and her father taught her how to select the freshest ingredients at the market and to prepare them simply in the Abruzzo style.

Still a adherent of Abruzzese cooking, Silvana La Rocca offers three meals featuring dishes and ingredients popular in that region. In Menus 1 and 2 she flavours the entrées, chicken and sole, respectively, with olive oil, garlic, and black pepper – all typical Abruzzese seasonings. She adds white wine and rosemary to the chicken and heightens the flavour of the tomato sauce for the sole with capers. The fish recipe is named for her grandmother.

In Menu 3 she features lamb chops that in Italy are called *agnello brucialingua*, or 'lamb that burns the tongue,' because they are fried with hot chili peppers. According to the cook, the accompanying potatoes (potato wedges baked in their skins with onions and carrots) are often prepared by Abruzzese hunters on trips to the mountains. The green bean and mint salad is a refreshing counterpoint to the spicy lamb.

Note: In all these recipes, tablespoon measurements are level tablespoons unless otherwise stated.

Fresh flowers and a richly patterned cloth set a festive tone for this colourful dinner. Golden-brown chicken pieces tossed with strips of red pepper are the appetizing entrée. Serve the cheese-and-herb-filled porcini mushroom caps and the radicchio and mozzarella salad in separate pottery dishes.

Stuffed Porcini Mushrooms
Chicken with Peppers
Radicchio and Mozzarella Salad

Large-capped meaty *funghi porcini*, called pigs' mushrooms because pigs love their flavour, are prized in Italy as a delicacy. Because *porcini* have a short growing season and are highly perishable, fresh ones may be difficult to locate at a greengrocer or an Italian market. As a substitute, use very large white cultivated mushrooms. Buy mushrooms that are fresh looking, unblemished, and have tightly fitting caps with no gills showing. Mushrooms will keep briefly in the refrigerator in a bowl covered with a damp towel, but they are best used the same day they are bought. Never wash or soak mushrooms; they absorb water and lose their flavour. Simply wipe them clean with a damp paper towel.

What to drink
Choose a full-bodied, very dry white wine such as an Italian Greco di Tufo or Pinot Bianco, or a California Pinot Blanc, for this northern Italian menu.

Start-to-Finish Steps
1 Squeeze lemon juice for mushrooms and salad recipes. Wash parsley and fresh herbs, if using, dry with paper towels, and set aside. Peel garlic for chicken and mushrooms recipes.
2 Follow salad recipe steps 1 through 3.
3 Follow mushrooms recipe steps 1 through 7.
4 Follow chicken recipe steps 1 through 5.
5 While chicken is browning, follow mushrooms recipe step 8 and salad recipe step 4.
6 Follow chicken recipe steps 6 through 8.
7 While chicken bakes, follow mushrooms recipe step 9 and serve as an appetizer.
8 Follow salad recipe step 5, chicken recipe step 9, and serve.

Stuffed Porcini Mushrooms

4 large fresh porcini mushrooms, or 4 extra-large cultivated mushrooms (about 125 g (4 oz) total weight)
Small bunch fresh parsley
60 g (2 oz) Parmesan cheese, preferably imported
60 g (2 oz) tin flat oil-packed anchovy fillets
1 clove garlic, peeled
4 fresh basil leaves, or 1 tablespoon dried

2 tablespoons lemon juice
1 teaspoon freshly ground black pepper
4 tablespoons olive oil

1 Preheat oven to 190°C (375°F or Mark 5).
2 Wipe mushrooms with damp cloth or paper towel. Carefully remove stems and reserve. Place mushrooms cap-side down in small baking dish; set aside.
3 Remove stems from parsley, and coarsely chop enough sprigs to measure 15 g (½ oz). Reserve remaining sprigs for garnish, if desired.
4 Using food processor or grater, grate enough Parmesan to measure 30 g (1 oz).
5 Drain 4 anchovy fillets and set aside; reserve oil and remaining fillets for another use.
6 In food processor or blender, combine mushroom stems, garlic, basil, anchovy fillets, Parmesan, lemon juice, parsley, and black pepper. Process 45 seconds. Scrape down sides of bowl and process another 30 seconds, or until mixture is medium-coarse.
7 Divide filling among mushroom caps, spoon 1 tablespoon olive oil over each mushroom, and set aside.
8 Place mushrooms in oven and bake 12 to 15 minutes, or until filling shrinks away slightly from sides of caps.
9 Transfer mushrooms to serving dish and garnish with parsley, if desired.

Chicken with Peppers

1.25–1.5 Kg (2½–3 lbs) chicken parts
125 g (4 oz) plain flour
Salt
2 sprigs fresh rosemary, or 1½ tablespoons dried
100 ml (3 fl oz) olive oil
2 to 3 cloves garlic, peeled
2 medium-size red bell peppers (about 250 g (8 oz) total weight)
125 ml (4 fl oz) dry white wine or dry vermouth
Freshly ground black pepper

1 Rinse chicken under cold running water and dry thoroughly with paper towels. Place flour in pie pan or plate. Sprinkle chicken with salt and lightly

dredge each piece in flour, coating evenly; shake off excess and set aside. Chop rosemary sprigs and set aside.

2 In large heavy-gauge skillet, heat olive oil over medium-high heat. Add garlic and sauté, stirring occasionally, 2 to 3 minutes, or until golden brown.

3 Remove garlic and discard. Place chicken in skillet in single layer, skin side down, increase heat to high, and sauté until one side is golden brown, 3 to 4 minutes.

4 While chicken is browning, halve, core, and seed bell peppers. Cut into 5 mm (1/4 inch) strips and set aside.

5 Turn chicken with tongs and sauté other side until evenly browned, 3 to 4 minutes. Meanwhile, lightly oil roasting pan.

6 Remove skillet from heat and transfer chicken pieces to roasting pan. Pour off fat from skillet, leaving about 2 tablespoons, and return skillet to medium heat. Add wine, increase heat to medium-high, and boil for 1 to 2 minutes, or until liquid is reduced by half.

7 Lower heat to medium, add bell pepper strips and rosemary, and cook, stirring, another 2 minutes.

8 Spoon bell pepper mixture over chicken pieces, sprinkle with freshly ground black pepper to taste, and bake, uncovered, in preheated 190°C (375°F or Mark 5) oven 15 minutes.

9 Transfer chicken and peppers to platter and serve.

Radicchio and Mozzarella Salad

2 to 3 heads radicchio (about 350 g (12 oz) total weight)
250 g (8 oz) fresh mozzarella, or good quality packaged mozzarella
7 fresh mint leaves, or 1/2 teaspoon dried
2 to 3 tablespoons lemon juice
100 ml (3 fl oz) olive oil
Salt and freshly ground black pepper

1 Wash radicchio and discard any bruised or wilted leaves. Dry with paper towels and place in salad bowl.

2 Cut cheese into thin 3 1/2 cm (1 1/2 inch) long strips and place on top of radicchio.

3 If using fresh mint, tear leaves into small pieces and sprinkle over salad. (If using dried, do not add at this point.) Cover bowl with plastic wrap and refrigerate until ready to serve.

4 In a small bowl, combine lemon juice, olive oil, and dried mint, if using. Add salt and pepper to

taste and, with fork, stir dressing until blended; set aside.

5 Just before serving, stir dressing to recombine, add to salad, and toss gently.

Added touch

For this dessert, select fresh figs that are medium-soft and that exude a drop of liquid from the rounded blossom end.

Fresh Figs in Monks' Robes

8 large fresh figs with smooth skins (about 750 g (1 1/2 lb) total weight)
8 blanched almonds
100 g (3 oz) unsweetened cocoa powder
175 g (6 oz) confectioners' sugar

1 Peel each fig carefully: Holding fig pointed end down, make shallow crosswise incision with paring knife just beneath skin at rounded end. Holding skin firmly against blade with your thumb, run knife under skin while gently pulling downward in the same motion. Repeat until all skin is removed.

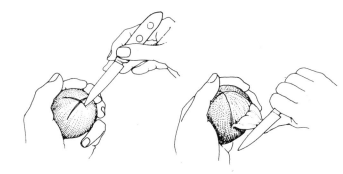

2 Press a whole blanched almond into bottom of each fig until totally enclosed.

3 Sift cocoa and sugar together into shallow dish.

4 Roll each fig in cocoa-sugar mixture until evenly coated.

5 Place figs on small platter, cover, and refrigerate for 15 to 20 minutes before serving.

Menu 2

Fillets of Sole Signora Concetta
Baked Onions
Fresh Tomato Salad

Special brine-cured olives garnish the sole fillets. The cook suggests using either tiny Italian Gaeta olives or Niçoise olives from France, which range in colour from brown to purple to black.

What to drink
The fresh, lively flavours of these dishes suggest a crisp, dry white wine as an accompaniment. A Verdicchio or Pinot Grigio would do very well, as would a California Sauvignon Blanc.

Start-to-Finish Steps
1 Follow onions recipe steps 1 and 2.
2 Follow sole recipe steps 1 and 2.
3 Follow onions recipe step 3.
4 While onion is cooking, follow salad recipe step 1.
5 Follow onions recipe step 4.
6 Follow sole recipe steps 3 and 4.
7 Follow onions recipe steps 5 and 6.
8 While onions bake, follow salad recipe step 2.
9 Follow sole recipe steps 5 through 9.
10 While sauce for sole is being reheated, follow onions recipe step 7 and salad recipe steps 3 and 4.
11 Follow sole recipe step 10, onions recipe step 8, and serve with salad.

Fillets of Sole Signora Concetta

2 cloves garlic, peeled and chopped
Small bunch fresh basil, or 2 teaspoons dried
500 g (1 lb) can plum tomatoes, drained
2 tablespoons capers

Sole fillets are crescents of baked onion look dramatic against solid black plates. The tomato salad adds extra colour.

125 ml (4 fl oz) olive oil
125 ml (4 fl oz) dry white wine or dry vermouth
Salt and freshly ground black pepper
4 medium-size fillets of sole
100 g (3 oz) plain flour
125 g (4 oz) Parmesan cheese
60 g (2 oz) small dark olives, preferably Gaeta or
   Niçoise

1 If using fresh basil, rinse and pat dry. Reserve 5 or
   6 leaves and refrigerate remainder for another use.
2 Coarsely chop enough tomatoes to measure 350 g
   (12 oz) reserving remainder for another use. Drain
   capers.
3 In medium-size non aluminium skillet, heat 4
   tablespoons olive oil over medium-high heat. Add
   garlic and sauté 2 to 3 minutes, or until golden.
4 Add tomatoes, basil, capers, and wine to skillet,
   and stir to combine. Raise heat to high and quickly
   bring sauce to a boil. Remove skillet from heat
   immediately, add salt and pepper to taste, and set
   aside.
5 Rinse fillets under cold water and dry with paper
   towels. Place flour on sheet of waxed paper.
   Sprinkle both sides of fillets with salt and pepper.
   Dredge fillets in flour, making sure each piece is
   well coated; shake off excess.
6 In large heavy-gauge non-aluminium skillet, heat
   remaining olive oil over medium-high heat. When
   oil is hot, add fillets, arranging in single layer, and
   lightly brown on one side, about 4 minutes.
7 Meanwhile, grate enough Parmesan to measure
   60 g (2 oz). Remove pits from olives; set aside.
8 Turn fish and brown another 4 minutes.
9 Return sauce to medium heat and warm 2 to 3
   minutes.
10 Divide fish among dinner plates. Top each fillet
   with hot tomato sauce, sprinkle with freshly grated
   Parmesan, and garnish with black olives.

Baked Onions

Extra-large onion (about 750 g (1¹/₂ lb))
1 tablespoon sugar
2 teaspoons fennel seeds
Salt and freshly ground white pepper
4 tablespoons olive oil
2 tablespoons white wine vinegar

1 Preheat oven to 200°C (400°F or Mark 6).
2 In large saucepan, bring 2¹/₂ ltrs (4 pts) water to a
   boil over high heat.

3 Cut off root end of onion and peel. Plunge onion
   into boiling water and boil 5 minutes.
4 Transfer onion to colander, drain, and set aside to
   cool.
5 Peel and quarter onion; cut quarters into thirds and
   arrange in single layer in baking dish. Sprinkle
   with sugar, fennel seeds, and salt and pepper to
   taste. Drizzle with olive oil and toss onions until
   coated.
6 Bake 30 to 35 minutes, or until onions are light
   golden.
7 Remove from oven and allow to cool 5 to 6
   minutes.
8 Sprinkle onions with vinegar and divide among
   plates.

Fresh Tomato Salad

4 large tomatoes (about 1¹/₂ Kg (3 lb) total weight),
   washed
4 scallions, washed, trimmed, and chopped
5 sprigs parsley, washed and chopped
Large lemon, washed
1 teaspoon dried oregano
Salt and freshly ground black pepper
125 ml (4 fl oz) olive oil

1 Cut tomatoes into eighths or narrow wedges and
   place in large bowl. Add scallions and parsley to
   tomatoes.
2 Holding lemon over bowl with tomatoes, remove
   zest, allowing it to fall into bowl.
3 Cut lemon in half and squeeze enough juice to
   measure 3 tablespoons; add to tomatoes.
4 Season tomatoes with oregano and salt and pepper
   to taste, drizzle with olive oil, and toss gently.
   Adjust seasoning, toss again, and divide among
   individual salad plates.

Menu 3

Spicy Lamb Chops
Hunter-style Potatoes
Green Beans with Mint

For the lamb recipe, use fresh hot chilies. Take special care when handling chilies; they contain a highly irritating substance that can burn the skin or cause a rash. Wear thin rubber gloves while working with chilies. After removing the gloves, do not touch your face until you have thoroughly washed your hands with soap and warm water.

What to drink

You will need a sturdy red wine to stand up to the lamb. A Chianti Classico Riserva would be ideal, or try an Italian Taurasi or a California Cabernet Sauvignon.

Start-to-Finish Steps

1 Prepare fresh herbs, if using.
2 Follow potatoes recipe steps 1 and 2.
3 Follow green beans recipe steps 1 through 3.
4 Follow potatoes recipe steps 3 and 4.
5 Follow green beans recipe step 4 and lamb recipe steps 1 through 5.
6 Follow potatoes recipe step 5 and green beans recipe steps 5 and 6.
7 Follow lamb recipe step 6.
8 Follow potatoes recipe step 6, lamb recipe step 7, and serve with green beans.

Serve each of your guests a lamb chop garnished with a chili pepper and sage, some roasted vegetables, and a bean salad.

12

Spicy Lamb Chops

4 fresh hot chili peppers, or 1$\frac{1}{2}$ to 3 tablespoons red pepper flakes
2 to 4 cloves garlic, peeled
125 ml (4 fl oz) olive oil
Four 3 cm (1$\frac{1}{4}$ inch) thick loin lamb chops (about 750 g (1$\frac{1}{2}$ lb) total weight)
6 to 8 fresh sage leaves, chopped, or $\frac{1}{2}$ teaspoon dried
2 tablespoons white wine vinegar
Salt and freshly ground black pepper
125 ml (4 fl oz) dry white wine or dry vermouth

1 If using fresh chili peppers, rinse under cold running water and dry with paper towels. Wearing rubber gloves, halve peppers lengthwise, remove seeds, and discard.
2 In large heavy-gauge skillet, heat olive oil over medium-high heat. Add chili peppers and garlic, and sauté 2 to 3 minutes, or until garlic is golden. Discard garlic.
3 Add lamb chops to skillet with chili peppers and brown over medium-high heat 3 to 4 minutes on one side.
4 Turn chops and brown another 3 to 4 minutes.
5 Add sage, vinegar, and salt and pepper to taste. Lower heat to medium, turn chops, and cook, uncovered, 8 minutes for rare, 10 for medium, or 12 for well done.
6 Add wine, raise heat to high, and cook chops another 3 to 5 minutes, or until most of wine has evaporated.
7 Divide chops among dinner plates, top each with a spoonful of pan juice, and serve.

Hunter-style Potatoes

4 medium-size boiling potatoes (about 750 g (1$\frac{1}{2}$ lb) total weight)
4 medium-size carrots (about 500 g (1 lb) total weight)
2 medium-size yellow onions (about 500 g (1 lb) total weight)
8 cloves garlic
1 tablespoon dried rosemary
Salt and freshly ground black pepper
4 tablespoons olive oil

1 Preheat oven to 200°C (400°F or Mark 6).
2 Wash and dry potatoes; cut into 2$\frac{1}{2}$ cm (1 inch) thick wedges. Trim and peel carrots. Halve carrots lengthwise, then cut into 2$\frac{1}{2}$ cm (1 inch) long strips. Peel and quarter onions.
3 Combine vegetables in baking dish. Add whole, unpeeled garlic cloves, rosemary, and salt and pepper to taste. Drizzle vegetables with olive oil and toss until well coated.
4 Roast potatoes in upper third of oven 15 minutes.
5 Remove dish from oven, turn vegetables, and return dish to oven. Roast another 15 minutes, or until potatoes are tender when pricked with a sharp knife.
6 Divide vegetables among dinner plates.

Green Beans with Mint

Salt
500 g (1 lb) green beans
1 lemon
10 to 12 fresh mint leaves, shredded, or 1 teaspoon dried
Freshly ground white pepper
100 ml (3 fl oz) olive oil

1 In stockpot or large kettle, bring 4$\frac{1}{2}$ ltrs (8 pts) of water and 1 tablespoon salt to a boil over high heat.
2 Meanwhile, snap off ends of beans and discard. Wash beans in cold running water and set aside. Squeeze enough lemon to measure about 3 tablespoons juice.
3 Add beans all at once to boiling water. When water returns to a boil, lower heat to medium-high and cook, uncovered, 7 minutes, or until beans are crisp-tender.
4 Turn beans into colander and refresh under cold running water. Drain and set aside until cool.
5 Dry beans thoroughly with paper towels and transfer to serving bowl. Add dried mint, if using, and white pepper to taste. Toss beans with olive oil until thoroughly coated. Add lemon juice, adjust seasoning, and toss again.
6 Add fresh mint, if using, and divide beans among individual salad plates.

Felice and Lidia Bastianich

Menu 1
(*left*)
Scampi with Quick Risotto
Asparagus Gratinati

Cooking comes naturally to Felice and Lidia Bastianich. As a youth he worked at his father's small northern Italian inn, and from the age of 14, she cooked for her entire family. Advocates of using only top-quality ingredients, the Bastianiches plan meals – both at home and in their restaurant – around what is best in the marketplace, then fill in with their own homemade prosciutto and pasta. By adhering to the unpretentious cooking traditions of their native Istria, the Bastianiches serve meals that are simple and nourishing. As Lidia Bastianich says, 'We want our customers and guests to be able to duplicate our recipes, so we stick to uncomplicated foods and methods.'

Istrian simplicity underlies each of the menus they present here. The sautéed shrimp of Menu 1 are lightly seasoned with garlic, lemon juice, and white wine, and are served on a bed of risotto. The asparagus spears are broiled with a light coating of melted butter and grated Parmesan.

In Istria, where game is abundant, cooks often serve polenta with wild fowl. Menu 2 offers quail in a tomato sauce flavoured with bay leaves, rosemary, and cloves, presented on a platter with polenta. A green bean and bacon salad adds colour and texture to this cold-weather meal.

Chicken is the entrée for Menu 3. The breasts are dredged with flour, dipped in parsley and grated Parmesan, and then sautéed in stock with wine and lemon juice. A substantial dish of Swiss chard and potatoes complements the fowl.

A heaping platter of risotto topped with whole shrimp in a garlic and parsley sauce is a delightful entrée for an informal spring dinner. The crisp-tender asparagus spears should be served on a warmed platter.

Scampi with Quick Risotto
Asparagus Gratinati

When buying raw shrimp, select those that are plump and odour-free; avoid any with meat that has shrunk away from the shell, which indicates that the shrimp have been frozen and thawed. If the shrimp do not have the shells and veins removed, follow step 1 of the recipe. Because they are highly perishable, shrimp should be purchased at the last minute. If you must store them, do so in a covered container in the coldest part of the refrigerator. After cooking, the shrimp should be firm and crisp.

What to drink

A well-chilled fruity white wine such as an Italian Chardonnay or Vernaccia, or a California Sauvignon Blanc or Riesling, goes well with the scampi.

Start-to-Finish Steps

1 Grate enough Parmesan to measure 1 cup for risotto recipe and ¹/₂ cup for asparagus recipe.
2 Follow scampi recipe steps 1 and 2.
3 Follow asparagus recipe steps 1 through 3 and scampi recipe step 3.
4 Follow asparagus recipe step 4 and risotto recipe steps 1 through 3.
5 Follow asparagus recipe steps 5 through 7.
6 Follow risotto recipe steps 4 and 5, and scampi recipe steps 4 through 6.
7 Follow asparagus recipe step 8 and scampi recipe step 7.
8 Follow risotto recipe step 6, scampi recipe step 8, and serve with asparagus.

Scampi with Quick Risotto

24 large shrimp (about 625 g (1¹/₄ lb) total weight)
4 cloves garlic
Small bunch parsley
1 lemon
3 tablespoons olive oil
4 tablespoons unsalted butter
125 ml (4 fl oz) dry white wine
Salt and freshly ground black pepper
3 tablespoons dry bread crumbs
Quick Risotto (see following recipe)

1 Pinch off legs of shrimp, several at a time, then bend back and snap off sharp, beak-like pieces of shell just above tail. Remove shell and discard. Using sharp paring knife, make shallow incision along back of each shrimp, exposing digestive vein. Extract vein and discard (see illustration).
2 Place shrimp in colander, rinse under cold running water, drain, and dry with paper towels. Set aside.
3 Peel and finely chop garlic. Rinse parsley, dry, and chop enough to measure 3 tablespoons. Squeeze enough lemon juice to measure 2 tablespoons; set aside.
4 In large heavy-gauge skillet, heat olive oil over medium-high heat. Add shrimp and sauté, stirring, about 2 minutes, or until slightly golden.
5 Stir in garlic and sauté 3 minutes, or until golden.
6 Add butter, lemon juice, white wine, and salt and pepper to taste, and cook about 5 minutes, or until shrimp begin to curl and turn opaque.
7 Sprinkle shrimp with parsley and bread crumbs, and cook another minute.
8 Turn shrimp and sauce onto platter with risotto.

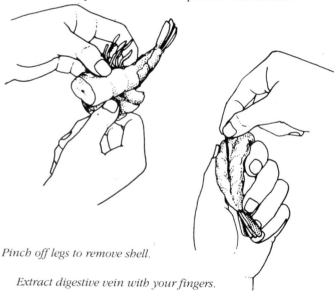

Pinch off legs to remove shell.

Extract digestive vein with your fingers.

Quick Risotto

Medium-size yellow onion
2 tablespoons olive oil
350 g (12 oz) long-grain rice

4 tablespoons unsalted butter
750 ml–1¹/₄ ltrs (1¹/₂–2 pts) chicken stock
Salt and freshly ground black pepper
125 g (4 oz) freshly grated Parmesan cheese

1 Peel and chop onion.
2 In large heavy-gauge saucepan, heat oil over medium-high heat. Add onion and sauté 5 minutes, or until golden.
3 Stir in rice, butter, 750 ml (1¹/₂ pts) chicken stock, and salt and pepper to taste. Reduce heat to low, cover, and cook, stirring occasionally, 10 minutes. If rice sticks to pan, add small amounts of stock, stirring after each addition until incorporated.
4 After 10 minutes, remove cover and allow excess stock to boil off; or, if rice seems too dry, add small amounts of stock, cover, and continue simmering another 5 to 10 minutes, or until rice is tender and all liquid is absorbed. Keep pan covered until ready to serve.
5 Meanwhile, place serving platter under hot running water to warm.
6 When ready to serve, dry platter. Add Parmesan to rice and stir until combined. Turn out onto warm platter.

Asparagus Gratinati

16 medium-size asparagus spears (about 500 g (1 lb) total weight)
2 tablespoons unsalted butter
60 g (2 oz) freshly grated Parmesan cheese

1 In stockpot or large saucepan, bring 1¹/₄ ltrs (2 pts) of water to a boil over high heat.
2 Meanwhile, rinse asparagus under cold running water and drain. Trim off woody stems and, if desired, peel.
3 Using kitchen string, tie asparagus into 2 bundles. Stand upright in pot, cover, and cook over high heat 6 minutes, or until crisp-tender.
4 With tongs, transfer bundles to colander, untie, and let cool.
5 In small heavy-gauge saucepan or butter warmer, melt butter over low heat.
6 In flameproof baking dish, arrange asparagus spears side by side in single layer and drizzle with melted butter. Sprinkle with Parmesan and set aside.
7 Preheat broiler.
8 Before serving, broil asparagus about 4 inches from heating element 3 to 5 minutes, or just until cheese turns light golden.

Added touch
When you ignite the warmed brandy Grand Marnier to flambé the strawberries, the flames may be high at first but should die down quickly. If they do not subside, simply put a cover on the skillet.

Flamed Strawberries

500 g (1 lb) fresh strawberries
Large orange
250 ml (8 fl oz) heavy cream
60 g (2 oz) sugar
2 tablespoons Grand Marnier or other orange liqueur
2 tablespoons brandy
500 ml (1 pt) vanilla ice cream

1 Place medium-size bowl and beaters in freezer to chill.
2 Rinse strawberries and pat dry with paper towels. With sharp paring knife, hull berries and set aside.
3 Rinse orange and dry. Grate enough rind to measure about 3 tablespoons. Cut orange in half. Squeeze juice from one half, reserving remaining half for another use.
4 Pour heavy cream into chilled bowl and whip with electric mixer at high speed until stiff. Cover and refrigerate.
5 In small heavy-gauge skillet, heat sugar over medium heat, stirring, until melted and golden, about 5 minutes.
6 Stir orange rind into sugar and cook about 2 minutes, or until sugar is light brown and syrupy.
7 Add strawberries, orange juice, Grand Marnier, and brandy, and stir to combine. Simmer gently, turning berries to coat with syrup, another 3 minutes.
8 Remove skillet from heat and, averting your face, ignite syrup. When flames have subsided, set skillet aside.
9 Place a generous spoonful of whipped cream in centre of each of 4 dessert plates. Top each with a scoop of ice cream and surround 'islands' with strawberries. Spoon remaining syrup over ice cream and serve.

Quail with Polenta
Green Bean, Red Onion, and Bacon Salad

A popular game bird considered a delicacy throughout the world, quail has pale-coloured flesh that tastes like a gamey version of dark-meat chicken. Fresh quail are now available year-round at many butchers. When buying quail, select those that are plump and silky-skinned with no discolouration.

What to drink
For this cold-weather meal, the cooks suggest a full-bodied red Barolo or Barbaresco from the Italian Piedmont or a Merlot from Friuli. California Merlot is a good domestic alternative.

Start-to-Finish Steps
1 Coarsely chop bacon for quail and salad recipes.
2 Follow salad recipe steps 1 through 3.
3 Follow quail recipe steps 1 and 2.
4 Follow salad recipe step 4 and polenta recipe steps 1 and 2.
5 Follow quail recipe steps 3 through 5.
6 While quail browns, follow salad recipe steps 5 through 8.
7 Follow quail recipe steps 6 and 7.
8 Follow polenta recipe steps 3 through 5.
9 Follow quail recipe step 8 and serve with polenta and salad.

Quail with Polenta

2 medium-size yellow onions (about 500 g (1 lb) total weight)
Small bunch fresh rosemary, or $1/2$ teaspoon dried
125 ml (4 fl oz) olive or vegetable oil
2 slices bacon, coarsely chopped
4 cloves
3 bay leaves
Salt
Freshly ground black pepper
8 quail (about 1.75 Kg ($3^1/2$ lb) total weight)
60 g (2 oz) Parmesan cheese (optional)
2 teaspoons tomato paste
250 ml (8 fl oz) dry white wine
500 ml (1 pt) chicken stock
Polenta (see following recipe)

Arrange the sautéed quail attractively around the polenta and garnish with a sprig of parsley, if desired; extra sauce may be served on the side. Bacon and red onion rings add colour to the green beans.

1 Peel and dice onions. Rinse fresh rosemary and pat dry with paper towels. Chop enough to measure 1 teaspoon.
2 In large heavy-gauge skillet, heat oil over medium heat. Add onions, rosemary, bacon, cloves, bay leaves, and salt and pepper to taste, and sauté, stirring occasionally, 5 to 10 minutes, or until onions are nicely browned.
3 Add quail and brown 8 to 10 minutes on one side.
4 If using Parmesan, grate enough in food processor or with grater to measure 30 g (1 oz); set aside.
5 Turn birds and cook another 8 to 10 minutes on other side, or until evenly browned.
6 In small bowl, blend tomato paste and wine. Add mixture to skillet and stir into pan juices until blended, basting birds as you stir. Raise heat to medium-high and simmer until liquid has almost evaporated, about 12 minutes.
7 Add stock and simmer another 15 minutes, or until tip of knife easily penetrates breast and juices run clear.
8 Transfer birds to platter with polenta. Pour sauce through strainer set over sauceboat or small bowl, extruding as much liquid as possible with back of spoon. Spoon sauce over each bird and around polenta. Sprinkle birds with cheese, if using, and serve with remaining sauce.

Polenta

125 g (4 oz) coarsely ground cornmeal
$^1/_2$ teaspoon salt
3 tablespoons unsalted butter
4 or 5 bay leaves

1 Preheat oven to 100°C (200°F or SLOW).
2 In large heavy-gauge saucepan, bring 1 ltr ($1^3/_4$ pts) water to a boil over high heat.
3 Place serving platter in oven to warm.
4 Reduce heat under saucepan to medium and add cornmeal in a very slow, steady stream, stirring constantly with wooden spoon. Add salt, butter, and bay leaves, and continue stirring until polenta thickens and pulls away from sides of pan, about 15 minutes.
5 Remove bay leaves and discard. With rubber spatula, turn out polenta into middle of warm platter.

Green Bean, Red Onion, and Bacon Salad

500 g (1 lb) green beans
Small red onion
4 slices bacon, coarsely chopped
3 tablespoons white or red wine vinegar
3 tablespoons olive or vegetable oil, approximately
Salt and freshly ground black pepper

1 In medium-size saucepan, bring $2^1/_2$ ltrs (4 pts) of water to a boil over high heat.
2 Meanwhile, trim beans. Peel red onion and cut into thin slices. Separate into rings and set aside.
3 Add beans to boiling water, lower heat to medium, cover, and cook 5 minutes, or just until crisp-tender.
4 Turn beans into colander and refresh under cold running water. Drain and set aside to cool.
5 In small skillet, cook bacon over medium heat, stirring occasionally, 5 minutes, or until crisp.
6 Meanwhile, transfer beans to large bowl.
7 Remove skillet from heat and pour off bacon fat. Add vinegar, stir, and return to heat for 1 minute.
8 Pour bacon and vinegar mixture over beans, add oil and salt and pepper to taste, and toss until combined. Adjust seasoning, toss again, and arrange on serving platter. Top with onion rings and set aside until ready to serve.

<table>
<tr><td>

Menu

3

</td><td>

Chicken Felice
Swiss Chard and Potatoes

</td></tr>
</table>

The lemony, cheese-encrusted boneless chicken breasts are simple to prepare and are an impressive dinner for company. The vegetable dish of Swiss chard and coarsely mashed potatoes can be varied if you wish: Substitute spinach or savoy cabbage for the chard.

For the best flavour, you should always buy Parmesan cheese by the chunk and grate it at home as needed. Slice off the rind before grating. If you are using a food processor to grate the cheese, cut the cheese into 1 cm (^{1}/$_2$ inch) cubes before grating with the steel blade.

What to drink
A dry, lightly acidic white Pinot Grigio, Gavi, or Verdicchio would be good here, or choose a domestic Sauvignon Blanc or fully dry Chenin Blanc.

Start-to-Finish Steps
1 Follow Swiss chard recipe steps 1 through 4.
2 Follow chicken recipe steps 1 through 3.
3 Follow Swiss chard recipe step 5.
4 Follow chicken recipe steps 4 through 6.
5 Follow Swiss chard recipe step 6.
6 Follow chicken recipe steps 7 through 10.
7 Follow Swiss chard recipe steps 7 through 10.
8 Follow chicken recipe steps 11 and 12 and Swiss chard recipe step 11.
9 Follow chicken recipe steps 13 and 14, and serve with Swiss chard and potatoes.

Chicken Felice

4 tablespoons unsalted butter
Small bunch parsley
60 g (2 oz) Parmesan cheese
4 skinless, boneless chicken breasts (about 750 g (1^1/$_2$ lb) total weight), halved and pounded 5 mm (^{1}/$_4$ inch) thick
4 eggs

Crisp golden chicken breasts topped with a lemon and wine sauce are accompanied by Swiss chard mashed with potatoes.

20

4 tablespoons milk
Salt and freshly ground black pepper
125 ml (4 fl oz) vegetable oil
125 g (4 oz) plain flour
3 lemons
250 ml (8 fl oz) dry white wine
750 ml (1¹/₂ pts) chicken stock

1   Preheat oven to 100°C (200°F or SLOW). Set out butter to reach room temperature.
2   Wash and dry parsley; chop enough to measure 2 tablespoons and refrigerate remainder for another use. In food processor fitted with steel blade, or with grater, grate enough cheese to measure 60 g (2 oz); set aside.
3   Rinse chicken and dry with paper towels.
4   Beat eggs in medium-size bowl. Add milk, grated cheese, chopped parsley, and salt and pepper to taste, and stir to combine.
5   In large heavy-gauge skillet, heat vegetable oil over medium-high heat until hot but not smoking.
6   Place flour in pie pan. One by one, dredge each breast lightly with flour, shake off excess, and dip in egg and cheese mixture, letting excess mixture drip off into bowl. Place coated breasts in skillet and fry 5 minutes on one side, or until golden.
7   Meanwhile, line heatproof platter with double thickness of paper towels. Rinse 2 lemons and dry. Cut each lemon into rounds, then halve, and set aside. Squeeze enough juice from remaining lemon to measure 2 tablespoons.
8   With tongs, turn breasts and fry another 5 minutes on other side, or until golden.
9   Transfer chicken to paper-towel-lined platter, loosely cover with foil, and keep warm in oven.
10 Pour off oil from skillet. Add wine, lemon juice, stock, and salt and pepper to taste to skillet and bring to a boil over medium-high heat. Continue boiling until sauce is reduced to about 250 ml (8 fl oz), about 10 to 15 minutes.
11 Place 4 dinner plates in oven to warm.
12 Reduce heat under skillet to medium. Return chicken to skillet and simmer 15 minutes.
13 Transfer chicken to warm plates. Add butter, 1 tablespoon at a time, to liquid in pan, swirling after each addition until butter is incorporated.
14 Remove pan from heat. Top each breast with a generous spoonful of sauce and garnish with lemon slices.

Swiss Chard and Potatoes

2 bunches Swiss chard (about 2 Kg (4 lb) total weight)
3 medium-size potatoes (about 625 g (1¹/₄ lb) total weight)
4 cloves garlic
4 tablespoons olive oil
3 tablespoons unsalted butter
Salt and freshly ground black pepper

1   In stockpot or large kettle, bring 7 ltrs (12 pts) of water to a boil over high heat.
2   Meanwhile, trim off lower (stem) half of Swiss chard. Cut leaf tops into 2¹/₂ cm (1 inch) pieces and wash thoroughly in several changes of cold water to remove all traces of grit.
3   Peel and quarter potatoes.
4   Add potatoes to boiling water and cook 5 minutes.
5   Add Swiss chard to potatoes and cook another 10 minutes.
6   Transfer vegetables to colander and drain.
7   Bruise garlic cloves with flat side of knife blade and peel.
8   In large heavy-gauge saucepan, heat oil over medium heat. Add garlic and sauté, stirring occasionally, until browned, 2 to 3 minutes.
9   Add Swiss chard, potatoes, butter, and salt and pepper to taste, and mash coarsely.
10 Cook mixture, stirring constantly with wooden spoon, 5 minutes.
11 Remove garlic cloves and discard. Turn vegetables into large heatproof bowl and keep warm in SLOW oven until ready to serve.

Lynne Kasper

Menu 1
(*right*)
Escarole, Onion, and Coppa Salad
Peasant-style Risotto

Lynne Kasper began her food career studying classic French theory and technique. but has amplified her food knowledge by researching Italian cuisine and history in Europe. Well versed in Italian cooking methods, she nonetheless describes herself as an interpretive cook who likes to vary traditional recipes but still preserve the essence of the originals.

For the risotto of Menu 1, a mainstay of the northern Piedmontese winter diet, she short-cuts the standard lengthy cooking process by covering the risotto while it cooks and stirring it only to prevent sticking. The result is still delicious and creamy.

Menu 2 is in the Renaissance style: The almond broth and broiled leg of lamb both incorporate the sweet, spicy, and savoury flavours loved by sixteenth-century cooks. However, Lynne Kasper serves the lamb rare to medium-rare rather than in the traditionally favoured well-done style. Roasted potatoes go well with the lamb.

Menu 3, a country-style meal that is good on a chilly autumn or winter day, features a first course of prosciutto with *mostarda di Cremona*, a spicy fruit relish imported from Cremona in Lombardy. The main course is a rich minestrone from the Marches region, served with crusty Italian bread.

Serve your guests the refreshing escarole, red onion, and coppa salad as a first course, and while they are enjoying it, finish preparing the peasant-style risotto.

Escarole, Onion, and Coppa Salad
Peasant-style Risotto

The light prelude to this substantial meal is a simple salad of escarole, onion, and *coppa*. A member of the endive family, escarole has a bushy head with broad, slightly curled, dark green leaves. If you plan to store the escarole for several days before using it, leave the head intact, place it in a plastic bag, and store in the refrigerator; wash just before using. You may wish to vary this salad by adding chopped bell peppers, marinated mushrooms, and quartered artichoke hearts. To dress the salad, the cook suggests a flavourful extra-virgin olive oil, particularly one from Tuscany or Liguria.

What to drink
The hearty main dish needs a medium-bodied red wine with a good flavour. The cook likes Barbera d'Alba, but a Barbera d'Asti, a Dolcetto, or a California Zinfandel is also fine.

Start-to-Finish Steps
1 Rinse fresh herbs, if using, and pat dry with paper towels. Chop basil for salad recipe; chop enough marjoram to measure 2 teaspoons for risotto recipe.
2 Follow risotto recipe steps 1 through 9.
3 While rice is cooking, follow salad recipe steps 1 through 3.
4 Follow risotto recipe steps 10 through 12.
5 While risotto is resting, follow salad recipe steps 4 and 5 and serve.
6 Follow risotto recipe steps 13 and 14, and serve.

Escarole, Onion, and Coppa Salad

Medium-size head escarole
Medium-size red onion
60 g (2 oz) sliced sweet coppa or capocollo
30 g (1 oz) sliced hot coppa or capocollo
6 tablespoons extra-virgin olive oil, approximately
2 tablespoons good-quality red or white wine vinegar, approximately
8 fresh basil leaves, chopped, or $1/2$ teaspoon dried, approximately
Salt
Freshly ground black pepper

1 Remove any tough or bruised outer leaves from escarole. Wash escarole and dry in salad spinner or with paper towels. Tear into bite-sized pieces and place in large salad bowl.
2 Peel and thinly slice onion. Add to escarole, cover bowl with plastic wrap, and refrigerate until ready to serve.
3 Coarsely chop coppa or capocollo; set aside.
4 Just before serving, add olive oil, vinegar, basil, and salt and pepper to taste. Toss salad to combine, taste, and adjust seasoning, adding more oil or vinegar, if desired.
5 Add coppa or capocollo to salad and toss to combine.

Peasant-style Risotto

2 medium-size carrots (about 350 g (12 oz) total weight)
2 medium-size yellow onions (about 500 g (1 lb) total weight)
Small head cabbage (about 500 g (1 lb))
625 g ($1^{1}/4$ lb) mild home-style Italian sausage
2 tablespoons vegetable oil
250 g (8 oz) canned Italian plum tomatoes
Large clove garlic
2 bay leaves
1 sprig fresh rosemary, or $1/2$ teaspoon dried
2 teaspoons fresh marjoram, chopped, or $1/2$ teaspoon dried
$1^{1}/4$ ltr (2 pts) chicken or beef stock, approximately
500 g (1 lb) canned pinto beans
175 ml (6 fl oz) dry red wine
250 g (8 oz) Italian Arborio rice
Salt and freshly ground black pepper

1 Peel carrots and cut into $2^{1}/2$ cm (1 inch) long pieces. Peel and quarter onions. Remove any tough or bruised outer leaves from cabbage. Core, halve, and quarter cabbage.
2 If using food processor, fit with steel blade and process carrots until reduced to small pieces. Remove carrots and coarsely chop cabbage. Remove cabbage, fit processor with slicing disc, and thinly slice carrots. Or, use chef's knife to coarsely chop carrots and cabbage, and to slice onions; set aside.

3 Cut sausage into 5 mm (¹/₄ inch) slices; set aside.

4 In large heavy-gauge non-aluminium saucepan, heat oil over medium-high heat. Add carrots, onions, and sausage, and cook, stirring frequently, until onions are golden, about 3 to 5 minutes. Reduce heat, if necessary, to prevent scorching.

5 While onions are cooking, drain 3 plum tomatoes and reserve remaining tomatoes and liquid for another use. Peel and mince garlic.

6 When onions are golden, tilt pan and spoon off all but about 4 tablespoons fat, if necessary. Stir in cabbage, tomatoes, garlic, bay leaves, and herbs, and cook, stirring frequently, over medium-high heat 3 to 4 minutes, or until aromatic.

7 Meanwhile, bring stock to a simmer in small saucepan over high heat. Turn beans into strainer, rinse under cold running water, and drain. Reduce heat under stock and keep hot.

8 Add wine and rice to vegetable-sausage mixture and bring to a boil, stirring to prevent rice from sticking.

9 Reduce heat under rice to medium, stir in 500 ml (1 pt) hot stock, cover pan, and cook, stirring occasionally to prevent sticking, about 10 minutes, or until stock is absorbed and mixture is creamy.

10 Add beans and 500 ml (1 pt) more hot stock to rice and cook, stirring occasionally, another 10 minutes, or until rice is *al dente* and consistency is quite creamy.

11 Remove risotto from heat, cover pan, and set aside to rest for about 15 minutes.

12 Preheat oven to SLOW and place heatproof serving bowl in oven to warm.

13 If after resting rice still tastes raw, add more stock, cover, and cook another few minutes until stock is absorbed.

14 Remove bay leaves and rosemary sprig, add salt and pepper to taste, and turn into warm serving bowl.

Added touch

These hazelnut meringues, a Piedmontese speciality known as bruti ma buoni ('ugly but good'), are an excellent dessert served with espresso.

Hazelnut Meringues

350 g (12 oz) shelled hazelnuts
175 g (6 oz) sugar
¹/₂ teaspoon cinnamon
4 egg whites, at room temperature
2 teaspoons unsalted butter
2 tablespoons plain flour, approximately

1 Preheat oven to 180°C (350°F or Mark 4).

2 Arrange nuts in single layer on large baking sheet and place in oven. Toast nuts, shaking pan occasionally to prevent nuts from scorching, 15 to 20 minutes, or until skins have split open and meat is light golden brown.

3 Remove nuts from oven and set aside. Reduce oven temperature to 130°C (250°F or Mark ¹/₂).

4 Remove skins from nuts by rubbing with clean kitchen towel. Transfer half of the nuts to food processor fitted with steel blade and chop coarsely. Turn chopped nuts into medium-size bowl. Process remaining nuts to a paste.

5 Add sugar, cinnamon, and nut paste to chopped nuts, and stir to combine.

6 In large copper or stainless-steel bowl, beat egg whites with electric beater at high speed, or with whisk, until soft peaks form.

7 Add nut mixture to egg whites and fold in until incorporated. Don't worry about the whites deflating.

8 Butter and flour a large cookie sheet; shake off excess flour.

9 Drop about 30 teaspoons batter onto sheet, spacing them about 2¹/₂ cm (1 inch) apart. Bake 1 hour to 1 hour and 10 minutes, or until firm and dry. When done, turn off oven but do *not* open oven door again.

10 Allow meringues to rest in oven 1 hour, then remove from oven, and cool to room temperature.

Bowls of almond broth precede the entrée of sliced lamb and roast potatoes garnished with fresh parsley.

Grilled butterflied leg of lamb flavoured with a butter that contains crushed juniper berries is an elegant main dish for a special dinner party. The meat of a butterflied leg has been carefully cut off the bone in one large piece so that it resembles a butterfly when laid out. Some sections of the butterflied leg will be thicker than others and will cook more slowly. Test for doneness in the thickest portion. Allow the lamb to rest for 15 minutes while you serve the soup.

Juniper berries, the dried blue fruit of small evergreen shrubs, are available in the spice section of most supermarkets. If you wish to intensify their bittersweet flavour, toast the berries lightly in a dry skillet for a minute or two, then crush them before adding them to the lamb filling.

Balsamic vinegar is a primary flavouring for the roast potatoes. Produced in the Modena province of the Emilia-Romagna region, this unique vinegar has a rich but not cloying flavour with woody and herbal overtones. It is delicious on salads and vegetables. Italian markets and speciality food shops sell this quality vinegar.

What to drink
A dry, fruity red wine suits this menu. The first choice would be a Dolcetto; good alternatives are a French Beaujolais or a California Gamay.

Start-to-Finish Steps

Thirty minutes ahead: Place chicken in freezer to chill.

1 Prepare fresh herbs, if using.
2 Follow potatoes recipe steps 1 through 4.
3 Follow lamb recipe steps 1 through 3.
4 Follow soup recipe steps 1 through 3.
5 Follow lamb recipe step 4.
6 Follow potatoes recipe step 5 and lamb recipe step 5; potatoes will roast while lamb grills.
7 Follow soup recipe steps 4 and 5, and lamb recipe step 6.
8 Follow soup recipe step 6.
9 Follow lamb recipe step 7 and potatoes recipe step 6.
10 Follow soup recipe step 7 and serve.
11 Follow lamb recipe step 8 and potatoes recipe step 7 and serve together.

Renaissance Almond Broth

1 ltr (1³/₄ pts) homemade chicken stock
Small clove garlic
125 g (4 oz) blanched slivered almonds
Pinch of cinnamon
Small bunch fresh chives or scallions

60–100 g (2–3 oz) skinless, boneless chicken breast half, well chilled
Salt and freshly ground black pepper

1 In medium-size heavy-gauge non-aluminium saucepan, bring stock to a boil over medium-high heat.
2 Peel garlic and process with almonds and cinnamon in processor or blender until almonds are powdered.
3 As soon as stock comes to a boil, add almond mixture, cover pan, and remove from heat. Let soup steep, covered, about 30 minutes.
4 Wash and dry chives or scallions. Cut enough chives or scallion greens into 2¹/₂ cm (1 inch) lengths to measure 2 tablespoons and set aside; reserve remainder for another use.
5 About 10 minutes before serving, remove chicken from freezer. With very sharp carving knife, shave chicken into paper-thin slices, moving knife across the grain and away from you. Arrange slices in single layer on large flat plate and season with salt and pepper to taste.
6 About 5 minutes before serving, strain broth through a fine sieve or strainer set over a medium-size bowl, pressing solids with back of spoon to extract as much liquid as possible. Return soup to saucepan and bring to a simmer over medium heat. Adjust seasoning.
7 Just before serving, add chicken slices to soup (they will cook in soup) and immediately ladle into 4 small bowls. Garnish with chopped chives or scallions and serve.

Sweet and Savoury Grilled Lamb

2 large cloves garlic
Large orange
6 juniper berries
4 tablespoons unsalted butter
2 tablespoons dry vermouth
¹/₄ teaspoon chopped fresh rosemary, or ¹/₄ teaspoon dried, plus 4 sprigs for garnish (optional)
¹/₄ teaspoon ground cloves
¹/₂ teaspoon freshly ground black pepper
Pinch of salt
3 large shallots
1.5 Kg (3 lb) loin half of leg of lamb, boned, butterflied, and trimmed

1 Peel and mince garlic. With zester, grate orange rind, reserving orange for another use. Crush juniper berries by placing them under flat blade of chef's knife and hitting blade sharply with heel of hand.

2 Combine all ingredients except shallots and lamb in small heavy-gauge non-aluminium saucepan and bring to a boil over medium heat. Reduce heat and simmer 2 minutes.

3 While butter-spice blend is simmering, peel and finely chop shallots. Stir shallots into butter, remove pan from heat, and allow to cool.

4 Place lamb on rack in grill pan. Using sharp paring knife, make about twelve $2^1/_2$–$3^1/_2$ cm (1–$1^1/_2$ inch) incisions at an angle, randomly spaced in surface of meat. Using a teaspoon, stuff incisions with butter mixture. Set lamb aside at room temperature.

5 Adjust grill pan so that lamb is about 10 cm (6 inches) from heating element, and grill 10 minutes.

6 For rare lamb, turn and grill another 5 minutes. For medium, grill another 2 to 3 minutes.

7 Turn off grill, leave oven door ajar, and let lamb rest about 15 minutes.

8 To serve, thinly slice lamb across grain. Divide slices among dinner plates and garnish each serving with a sprig of rosemary, if desired.

Herb-Roasted Potatoes

1 Kg (2 lb) small red-skinned new potatoes
8 leaves fresh sage, or 1 teaspoon dried
Salt and freshly ground black pepper
5 tablespoons extra-virgin olive oil
4 tablespoons balsamic vinegar
12 sprigs fresh parsley for garnish (optional)

1 Preheat oven to 220°C (425°F or Mark 7).

2 Wash potatoes thoroughly under cold running water but do not peel; dry with paper towels.

3 Place potatoes in roasting pan, sprinkle with whole sage leaves and salt and pepper to taste, and drizzle with olive oil. Toss potatoes until evenly coated with oil and seasonings.

4 Place pan on lower oven rack and roast 25 minutes, turning occasionally to prevent sticking.

5 Remove potatoes from oven and turn on broiler. Sprinkle potatoes with 3 tablespoons vinegar and return to oven to continue roasting 15 to 20 minutes.

6 Remove potatoes from oven and cover loosely with foil to keep warm until ready to serve.

7 Use slotted spoon to divide potatoes among dinner plates; sprinkle with remaining vinegar and garnish each serving with parsley sprigs, if desired.

Baked Courgettes and Tomatoes

3 medium-size courgettes (about 625 g ($1^1/_4$ lb) total weight)
6 plum or other small vine-ripened tomatoes (about 625 g ($1^1/_4$ lb) total weight)
4 tablespoons extra-virgin olive oil
Salt and freshly ground black pepper
30 g (1 oz) parsley sprigs
1 tablespoon chopped fresh basil, or 1 teaspoon dried
2 teaspoons fresh marjoram leaves, or $^1/_2$ teaspoon dried
Small clove garlic, peeled
$^1/_2$ small onion
1 cm ($^1/_2$ inch) thick slice stale Italian or French bread
1 tablespoon unsalted butter

1 Preheat oven to 200°C (400°F or Mark 6).

2 Wash courgettes and tomatoes, and dry with paper towels. Trim off ends from courgettes and discard. Cut courgettes on diagonal into 5 mm ($^1/_4$ inch) thick slices. Core tomatoes and cut into thin wedges.

3 Coat bottom and sides of medium-size heavy-gauge baking dish with 1 tablespoon olive oil. Arrange alternating slices of courgettes and tomatoes in rows, reversing slant of slices so that adjacent rows slant in opposite directions. Sprinkle with salt and pepper to taste and drizzle with 1 teaspoon olive oil.

4 Combine parsley, basil, marjoram, garlic, onion, bread, and butter in food processor or blender and process until finely minced. Do *not* overprocess. Season mixture to taste with salt and pepper.

5 Spread mixture over vegetables and drizzle with remaining olive oil. Bake about 45 minutes, or until courgettes can be pierced easily with tip of knife.

Prosciutto and Mostarda di Cremona
Minestrone with Chickpeas

For a quick supper, offer prosciutto with mostarda di Cremona *and then bowls of hearty minestrone with crusty bread.*

The elegant appetizer for this easy menu pairs delicate prosciutto with the spicy-sweet fruits of *mostarda di Cremona*. Sold in jars at speciality food shops, these fruits preserved in syrup are flavoured with yellow mustard seeds, spices, and sometimes mustard oil. Refrigerate them after opening, and eat them within a month. If *mostarda di Cremona* is unavailable, use whole fresh ripe figs or sweet pears instead.

Both dried Greek oregano and dried *porcini* mushrooms add flavour to the main-course soup. Greek oregano is milder and sweeter than the more commonly sold Mexican variety. Check the label for country of origin. Dried *porcini* mushrooms have a powerful flavour. Select those that are light coloured and not too crumbly; they store well for up to two years.

What to drink
To complement this hearty country fare, choose a rustic red wine such as a Sangiovese di Romagna or a red Lacryma Christi.

Start-to-Finish Steps
1 Follow minestrone recipe steps 1 through 6.
2 While vegetables are cooking, follow prosciutto recipe steps 1 through 3.
3 Follow minestrone recipe steps 7 through 12.
4 While pasta is cooking, follow prosciutto recipe steps 4 and 5.
5 Follow minestrone recipe step 13, prosciutto recipe step 6, if using pears, and serve prosciutto and fruits as first course.
6 Follow minestrone recipe step 14 and serve.

Prosciutto and Mostarda di Cremona

Small head lettuce
12 thin slices prosciutto (about 125 g (4 oz))
125 g (4 oz) candied mustard fruits, such as mostarda di Cremona, or 4 fresh ripe figs or 4 ripe Bartlett pears
1 lemon or lime (optional), plus additional lemon if using pears

1 Rinse lettuce and dry in salad spinner or with paper towels. Discard any blemished outer leaves. Reserve 4 leaves and refrigerate remainder for another use.
2 Roll each slice of prosciutto into a large cone. Arrange 3 cones on each serving plate, with points together in fan-like shape.
3 If using mustard fruits, select whole fruits in contrasting colours, such as a fig, apricot, or small pear; cut larger fruits into quarters. If using figs, peel carefully. If using pears, combine juice of 1 lemon and 1¼ ltrs (2 pts) cold water in large bowl. Peel pears, placing each in bowl as you finish peeling to prevent discolouration.
4 Place a lettuce leaf at the point of each prosciutto fan and top leaf with some mustard fruits, or with a whole peeled fig.
5 If mustard fruits are too sweet, halve lemon or lime and squeeze a little juice over each serving. Cover plates loosely with plastic wrap and set in cool place until ready to serve. Do not refrigerate.
6 If using pears, just before serving, drain and divide among plates.

Minestrone with Chickpeas

25 g (³/₄ oz) dried porcini mushrooms or cèpes
Small bunch fresh parsley
1 stalk celery with leaves
Small bunch fresh basil, or 2 teaspoons dried
Medium-size carrot
3 medium-size onions (about 500 g (1 lb) total weight)
2 large cloves garlic
1 pork loin chop (about 175 g (6 oz))
250 g (8 oz) smoked country-style bacon, sliced
3 tablespoons extra-virgin olive oil
175 g (6 oz) Parmesan cheese, preferably imported
³/₄ teaspoon dried oregano, preferably Greek
500 g (1 lb) canned chickpeas
300 g (10 oz) tomato purée
500 g (1 lb) canned Italian plum tomatoes
Medium-size courgette
175 g (6 oz) pickled sweet red peppers
1¹/₂ ltrs (2¹/₂ pts) homemade chicken stock
175 g (6 oz) pappardelle or other dry, flat, broad pasta
Salt and freshly ground black pepper

1   In small bowl, combine dried mushrooms with enough hot water to cover and set aside for at least 15 minutes.

2   Wash parsley, celery, and fresh basil, if using, and dry with paper towels. Reserve 15 g (¹/₂ oz) parsley; refrigerate remainder for another use. Chop enough basil to measure 2 tablespoons. Trim celery and cut into large pieces. Trim and peel carrot; cut into large pieces. Peel onions. Peel and mince garlic.

3   Remove bone from pork chop and discard; coarsely chop meat. Coarsely chop bacon.

4   Heat oil in large heavy-gauge non-aluminium saucepan or casserole over medium-high heat. Add bacon and chopped pork, and sauté, stirring frequently, 5 to 7 minutes or until golden.

5   Meanwhile, if using food processor, grate enough cheese to measure 175 g (6 oz) and transfer to small serving bowl. Or, using grater, grate cheese. Add celery and carrot, and process until medium-fine. With slicing disc, slice onions over vegetables. If using chef's knife, finely chop parsley, celery, and carrot, and thinly slice onions.

6   When meat is done, carefully spoon off all but 3 tablespoons of fat. Add vegetables, stirring to scrape up any brown bits clinging to bottom of pan. Cover, reduce heat to medium-low, and cook 10 minutes.

7   Add mushrooms and, using fine sieve or strainer lined with paper towel, strain soaking liquid into pan. Stir in minced garlic and herbs, and simmer gently 2 to 3 minutes, or until aromatic.

8   Meanwhile, turn chickpeas into sieve or strainer, rinse under cold running water, and drain; set aside.

9   Add tomato purée and plum tomatoes with their liquid to pan, bring to the boil, stirring, and simmer briskly 5 minutes.

10 Wash courgettes and dry. Trim off ends and discard; cut courgettes into 1 cm (¹/₂ inch) dice. Drain red peppers and rinse under cold running water. Pat dry with paper towels and cut into 5 mm (¹/₄ inch) wide strips.

11 Add chickpeas, courgettes, and red pepper strips to pan, and cook, stirring, 1 minute.

12 Stir in chicken stock and bring to a simmer. Add pasta and cook, stirring frequently, 6 to 8 minutes, or until pasta is tender but not mushy.

13 Season with salt and pepper to taste and remove pan from heat. Cover and allow to rest about 10 minutes.

14 If necessary, reheat soup briefly over medium heat before serving. To serve, divide among soup bowls, garnish each with a generous spoonful of Parmesan, and offer remaining cheese separately.

Susan DeRege

Menu 1
(*left*)
Piedmontese Pork Medallions
Straw and Hay Pasta with Butter Sauce
Carrots with Kirsch

Susan DeRege spends long hours in the kitchen almost daily as part of her job, yet she never tires of cooking at home for friends and family. She likes meals that can be prepared ahead, allowing her to spend time with her guests. The three menus she presents here are all based on the cooking of northern Italy.

The pork medallions and the glazed carrots in Menu 1, both Piedmont recipes, can be prepared early in the day, refrigerated, and then quickly reheated for the table. The straw and hay pasta – a recipe from Emilia-Romagna – should be prepared just before dinner.

Menu 3 is a favourite of this cook because it can be made a day ahead and is perfect for either a buffet or a sit-down dinner. The Ligurian artichoke soup is equally good chilled or heated, and the peppers can be served at room temperature or hot. The veal entrée, a Piedmont dish, is named for Count Cavour, the nineteenth-century statesman who came from the region.

Menu 2 is a bit more complicated. The creamy risotto requires constant stirring, so Susan DeRege suggests inviting your guests into the kitchen for a glass of wine while you prepare the meal. The risotto is bound with Parmesan cheese, which also flavours the accompanying Milanese-style chicken. In an Italian home, the endive salad would be served after the main course

Casual pottery underscores the simplicity of this family meal: pork medallions with a sweet and sour sauce and finger carrots glazed with fruity kirsch. The two-toned pasta dish, tossed with butter, is sprinkled with freshly grated Parmesan and black pepper.

Piedmontese Pork Medallions
Straw and Hay Pasta with Butter Sauce
Carrots with Kirsch

The yellow and green egg noodles may be served as the appetizer or as an accompaniment to the pork medallions and carrots. If the cooked pasta is too dry after adding the Parmesan, tossing the pasta with a little of the hot cooking water will improve the sauce.

The pork medallions simmer gently in milk flavoured with rosemary and vinegar. Soft curds may appear when you first add the vinegar to the milk, but after slow cooking they will almost disappear. If you want an especially smooth sauce, blend the milk mixture in your blender or food processor for a few seconds.

What to drink

A dry but not overpowering red wine, such as a Spanna or a Nebbiolo from the Italian Piedmont, would make the best partner for these dishes.

Start-to-Finish Steps

1 Follow pork recipe steps 1 through 3 and carrots recipe steps 1 and 2.
2 Follow pasta recipe steps 1 and 2.
3 Follow carrots recipe steps 3 and 4.
4 Follow pasta recipe steps 3 through 7.
5 Follow pork recipe step 4 and serve with pasta and carrots.

Piedmontese Pork Medallions

1 tablespoon virgin olive oil
1 tablespoon unsalted butter
750 g (1½ lb) boneless pork loin roast from the rib end, cut into 12 medallions and pounded 1 cm (½ inch) thick
Salt and freshly ground black pepper
350 ml (12 fl oz) milk
3 tablespoons balsamic vinegar
3 sprigs fresh rosemary, or 1½ teaspoons dried rosemary, crushed, plus 4 sprigs for garnish (optional)

1 Heat olive oil and butter in large heavy-gauge skillet over high heat. Place about half the medallions in skillet in a single layer and sauté about 3 minutes per side, or until brown. As they brown, transfer medallions to platter and season with salt and pepper to taste. Repeat process for remaining medallions.

2 Lower heat under skillet to medium-high. Add milk slowly to prevent boiling, stirring and scraping up any browned bits clinging to bottom of pan. Stir in vinegar and rosemary. Cover pan and bring liquid to a boil.

3 When liquid comes to a boil, reduce heat to low. Return all the medallions to skillet, cover partially, and cook, turning occasionally with tongs, 25 to 35 minutes, or until pork is fork-tender and sauce is caramel coloured and has reduced to 125 ml (4 fl oz).

4 Remove rosemary sprigs and discard. Divide medallions among plates and top each serving with sauce. Garnish each plate with a sprig of fresh rosemary, if desired.

Straw and Hay Pasta with Butter Sauce

60 g (2 oz) unsalted butter
1½ tablespoons salt
175 g (6 oz) green fettuccine plus 175 g (6 oz) white
125 g (4 oz) Parmesan cheese
Freshly ground black pepper

1 Bring 6 ltrs (10 pts) cold water to a boil over high heat in stockpot or large kettle. Preheat oven to SLOW and place 4 bowls in oven to warm.

2 While water is coming to a boil, cut butter into 8 pieces, transfer to large ovenproof bowl or casserole, and place in oven.

3 Add salt and pasta to boiling water and stir with wooden spoon to blend green and white noodles. Cook pasta 8 to 12 minutes, or just until *al dente*.

4 In food processor or with grater, grate enough Parmesan to measure 100 g (3 oz); set aside.

5 When pasta is almost cooked, remove 60 ml (2 fl oz) pasta water and reserve. Turn pasta into colander and drain.

6 Transfer pasta to bowl with melted butter and toss until well coated. Add pepper and 60 g (2 oz) Parmesan, and toss again. If pasta is still too dry,

add a little reserved pasta water and toss to combine.

7   Divide pasta among warm bowls, sprinkle each serving with Parmesan, and add a few twists of black pepper; serve remaining cheese separately.

Carrots with Kirsch

14–16 medium carrots, about 1.25 Kg (2$^1/_2$ lb) total weight
Small bunch fresh parsley
6 tablespoons butter
$^1/_2$ teaspoon salt
Freshly ground black pepper
$^1/_4$ cup kirsch

1   Trim and peel carrots. If using finger carrots, leave whole, or halve regular carrots lengthwise, cut crosswise into 5 cm (2 inch) pieces, then cut into 1 cm ($^1/_2$ inch) julienne. Wash parsley, dry, and chop enough to measure 2 tablespoons; set aside.
2   In medium-size skillet, bring 1 cm ($^1/_2$ inch) water to a boil over medium-high heat. Add carrots, cover, and cook 6 to 8 minutes, or until they are crisp-tender. Be careful not to let water boil away or carrots will burn.
3   Pour off any water remaining in skillet and lower heat to medium. Add butter, salt, pepper to taste, and kirsch; cook, shaking pan to dissipate alcohol, 3 to 4 minutes, or until carrots are glazed.
4   Turn carrots into medium-size ovenproof bowl, sprinkle with chopped parsley, and keep warm in SLOW oven until ready to serve.

Added touch
For this elegant dessert, ripe pears are served in a *zabaglione*, a foamy custard, and drizzled with melted semi-sweet chocolate.

Pears Contessa

4 egg yolks
125 g (4 oz) sugar
125 ml (4 fl oz) dry Marsala
Juice of 1 lemon
4 ripe pears with stems intact
125 ml (4 fl oz) heavy cream
60 g (2 oz) imported semi-sweet chocolate

1   Place medium-size bowl and beaters in freezer to chill.
2   Combine egg yolks and sugar in small heavy-gauge non-aluminium saucepan and whisk until thick and fluffy. Gradually add Marsala, whisking until blended.
3   Place saucepan over medium heat and whisk egg mixture briskly until it coats whisk and mounds slightly, about 7 minutes.
4   Turn zabaglione into stainless-steel mixing bowl, cover with plastic wrap, and place in freezer to chill, about 25 minutes.
5   Meanwhile, combine lemon juice and 1$^1/_4$ ltrs (2 pts) cold water in large mixing bowl. Peel pears, placing each in lemon water as you finish peeling it to prevent discolouration.
6   In chilled bowl, beat heavy cream with electric mixer at high speed until stiff. Fold about 60 ml (2 fl oz) of chilled zabaglione into the whipped cream, then fold in remaining zabaglione.
7   Pour zabaglione cream into centre of gently sloping bowl or 2 ltr (3 pt) soufflé dish. Arrange whole pears around edge, cover with plastic wrap, and refrigerate until ready to serve.
8   Just before serving, melt chocolate in top of double boiler over hot, not boiling, water.
9   Drizzle melted chocolate over pears and zabaglione, and divide among individual plates.

Chicken Breasts Milanese
Risotto with Porcini Mushrooms
Endive salad with Green Herb Sauce

Instead of using the traditional – and expensive – veal cutlets for this entrée, the cook prepares chicken breasts. However, you can use turkey breasts instead. Dipping the breasts into the seasoned beaten-egg mixture before coating them helps the bread crumbs and Parmesan adhere to the meat.

A good risotto requires patience – here you stir the rice continuously while slowly adding the broth. The trick is not to overcook the dense, creamy mixture because the risotto continues cooking even when removed from the heat.

The endive salad is dressed with a piquant green sauce *(bagnetto verde)*. The sauce is quickly prepared in a food processor or blender and keeps well in the refrigerator for up to a month.

What to drink
This menu deserves either a full-bodied white wine or a light-bodied red. For white, the cook suggests Fiano di Avellino; for red, Grignolino.

Start-to-Finish Steps
1 Prepare parsley, watercress, and fresh herbs, if using. Grate enough Parmesan to measure 1 cup and set aside.
2 Follow risotto recipe steps 1 and 2 and chicken recipe steps 1 through 3.
3 Follow salad recipe steps 1 through 3.
4 Follow herb sauce recipe steps 1 through 3.
5 Follow chicken recipe steps 4 through 6.
6 Follow risotto recipe steps 3 through 7.
7 Follow salad recipe step 4, chicken recipe step 7, and serve with risotto.

Chicken Breasts Milanese

1 lemon
2 eggs
60 g (2 oz) freshly grated Parmesan cheese
Salt and freshly ground black pepper

Crumb-coated chicken breasts, risotto with porcini *mushrooms, and an endive salad are a classic northern Italian meal.*

2 skinless, boneless chicken breasts (about 750 g
    (1½ lb) total weight), halved and trimmed
60 g (2 oz) dry white bread crumbs
3 tablespoons unsalted butter
4 tablespoons corn oil
1 sprig fresh rosemary, or ½ teaspoon dried
4 sprigs parsley for garnish (optional)

1   Rinse lemon and dry. Cut into 4 wedges and set
    aside.
2   In medium-size bowl, combine eggs, 30 g (1 oz)
    of the Parmesan, and salt and pepper to taste, and
    beat until well blended. Add chicken breasts to
    egg mixture, turn to coat, and set aside to soak
    about 10 minutes.
3   Combine remaining cheese and bread crumbs in
    pie pan; set aside.
4   Preheat oven to SLOW. Line heatproof serving
    platter with paper towels.
5   In large heavy-gauge skillet, heat butter, corn oil,
    and rosemary over medium-high heat.
6   While fat is heating, dredge each chicken piece in
    crumb-cheese mixture until evenly coated. When
    butter stops foaming, add chicken to pan and
    sauté 4 to 5 minutes per side, or until golden
    brown. Transfer to paper-towel-lined platter and
    keep warm in oven until ready to serve.
7   Remove paper towels from platter and garnish
    chicken with lemon wedges and parsley sprigs, if
    desired.

Risotto with Porcini Mushrooms

15 g (½ oz) dried porcini mushrooms
Small yellow onion
750 ml (1½ pts) combined chicken and beef stock
4 tablespoons unsalted butter
1 tablespoon corn oil
Pinch of dried rosemary
300 g (10 oz) Italian Arborio rice
2 tablespoons dry sherry
¼ teaspoon salt
60 g (2 oz) freshly grated Parmesan cheese

1   Rinse mushrooms under cold water. Place them in
    small bowl, cover with warm water, and soak 20
    minutes.
2   Peel and finely chop enough onion to measure 2
    tablespoons; set aside.
3   Place serving bowl in SLOW oven. Bring stock to
    a boil in medium-size saucepan over high heat,
    then reduce heat to just maintain a simmer.

4   While stock is heating, combine 3 tablespoons
    butter, oil, rosemary, and onion in large heavy-
    gauge saucepan or enamel-lined casserole over
    medium heat and sauté, stirring occasionally, 5 to
    8 minutes, or just until onions are translucent. Add
    rice and stir until translucent and well coated with
    fat; do not brown.
5   Lower heat slightly and add hot stock gradually,
    about 125 ml (4 fl oz) at a time, stirring constantly
    after each addition until stock is totally absorbed
    by rice. Add mushrooms and their soaking liquid
    to rice. Add sherry and continue stirring over
    medium-low heat until liquid is absorbed, about
    20 minutes.
6   When liquid is absorbed, stir in salt and 30 g (1 oz)
    Parmesan.
7   Remove pan from heat and stir in remaining
    tablespoon butter. Turn risotto into warm serving
    bowl and offer remaining cheese separately.

Endive salad with Green Herb Sauce

2 medium-size heads Belgian endive (about 250 g
    (8 oz) total weight)
Medium-size carrot
8 sprigs watercress
Green Herb Sauce (see following recipe)

1   Halve, core, and separate endive leaves. Wash
    thoroughly and dry with paper towels.

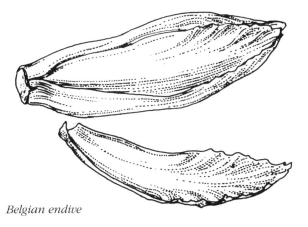

Belgian endive

2   Trim and peel carrot. Halve carrot lengthwise and
    cut halves into 5 cm (2 inch) pieces. Cut each piece
    into thin matchsticks.
3   Divide endive among individual salad plates and
    top with watercress. Sprinkle each serving with

carrot sticks, cover with plastic wrap, and refrigerate until ready to serve.

4 Just before serving, remove salads from refrigerator and place a generous spoonful of green herb sauce on each plate.

Green Herb Sauce

1 sprig fresh rosemary, or 1$\frac{1}{2}$ teaspoons dried
1 tablespoon capers
60 g (2 oz) fresh parsley
3 leaves fresh sage, or $\frac{1}{2}$ teaspoon dried
2 leaves fresh basil, or $\frac{1}{4}$ teaspoon dried
1 teaspoon dried thyme
1 teaspoon dried oregano
$\frac{1}{4}$ teaspoon chili powder
1 very large clove garlic
$\frac{1}{4}$ teaspoon salt
$\frac{1}{4}$ teaspoon freshly ground pepper
1 tablespoon red wine vinegar
4 tablespoons virgin olive oil
2 anchovies
4 tablespoons tomato sauce

1 Strip leaves from rosemary. Drain capers in small strainer and rinse under cold running water.
2 In food processor or blender, process all ingredients, except olive oil, anchovies, and tomato sauce, until finely chopped.
3 Add remaining ingredients and purée. Adjust seasoning and set aside at room temperature until ready to serve.

Added touch

For this version of the traditional Italian custard called *panna cotta*, or cooked cream, use a brioche pan to mould the dessert. This classic pan has fluted sides that flare outward from a small round base. Oil the pan before adding the hot custard to make unmoulding easier. If you do not have a brioche pan, a 1$\frac{1}{4}$ ltr (2 pt) soufflé dish or glass baking dish works well.

Moulded Caramel Custard

60 ml (2 fl oz) milk
125 g (4 oz) plus 3 tablespoons sugar
2 teaspoons unflavoured gelatin
4 egg yolks
Pinch of Salt
2 tablespoons praline liqueur or Cognac
350 ml (12 fl oz) heavy cream

1 Place bowl and beaters for whipping cream in freezer to chill.
2 In small heavy-gauge non-aluminium saucepan, heat milk over medium heat just until it begins to boil. Remove pan from heat.
3 In tea kettle or small saucepan, bring about 250 ml (8 fl oz) water to a boil.
4 In small heavy-gauge sauté pan, melt 125 g (4 oz) sugar over low heat, stirring constantly, 8 to 10 minutes, or until melted and straw coloured.
5 Remove pan from heat and *very* slowly add 2 tablespoons of the boiling water, stirring constantly, until water is incorporated. Return pan to low heat and cook another 5 minutes, or until caramel thickens.
6 Meanwhile, combine gelatin and 2 tablespoons cold water in small bowl and stir until gelatin dissolves.
7 In medium-size heavy-gauge saucepan, combine egg yolks, remaining sugar, and salt. Add a little hot water milk to yolks and stir until melted. Slowly stir in remainder of the milk and cook over low heat, about 5 minutes, or until mixture is thick enough to coat a spoon.
8 Stir in gelatin until incorporated. Stir in two thirds of the warm caramel mixture and the liqueur, cover, and chill in freezer 15 to 20 minutes, or until custard is consistency of stiffly beaten heavy cream.
9 Meanwhile, beat heavy cream until stiff, then gently fold into the chilled custard. Pour into an oiled brioche pan and chill at least 3 hours or overnight.
10 When ready to serve, dip bottom of mould briefly in warm water. Place flat serving plate upside down over pan, tap once sharply against hard surface, and, holding firmly together, invert. Remove pan, drizzle custard with remaining caramel, and serve.

Cream of Artichoke Soup
Veal Scallopini Cavour
Peperonata

For this meal the veal is coated evenly with flour, quickly sautéed, and then braised until tender. This technique allows you to use meat from the rump or lower part of the leg rather than expensive top round. The flour browns to a crust and also helps to thicken the braising liquid as the meat cooks. If you assemble all of the ingredients for the veal dish before heating the fat, you can put the meat right into the pan as you dredge the veal. Do not let the meat sit in the flour or the coating will become soggy and stick to the pan rather than to the meat.

For the Italian-style peppers, buy only red and yellow bell peppers that have a uniform, glossy colour and thick flesh; they should feel firm and heavy.

Refrigerated in a plastic bag, unwashed peppers keep for up to a week.

What to drink

A white Italian Gavi or top-quality Soave, or a red Dolcetto or Chianti Classico, are all good with veal.

Start-to-Finish Steps

One hour ahead: Set out frozen artichoke hearts to thaw for soup recipe.

1   Wash parsley and dry with paper towels. Reserve 4 parsley sprigs for soup garnish, if desired, and chop enough to measure 1 tablespoon for veal

The artichoke soup may be served before the entrée of braised veal and strips of sautéed red and yellow peppers.

39

recipe; refrigerate remainder for another use. Squeeze enough juice from 1 lemon to measure 3 tablespoons for veal recipe. If using lemon for soup garnish, rinse, dry, and cut remaining lemon crosswise into 8 very thin slices.

2   Follow soup recipe steps 1 through 3.
3   While soup is simmering, follow veal recipe steps 1 through 5 and set pan aside.
4   Follow soup recipe step 4 and peppers recipe steps 1 and 2.
5   Follow soup recipe steps 5 and 6.
6   Follow veal recipe step 6, peppers recipe step 3, and soup recipe step 7.
7   Follow peppers recipe step 4.
8   Follow soup recipe step 8 and serve as first course.

Cream of Artichoke Soup

Small yellow onion
500 g (1 lb) frozen artichoke hearts, thawed
350 ml (12 fl oz) milk
1 teaspoon salt
1 teaspoon sugar
2 eggs
250 ml (8 fl oz) heavy cream
Freshly ground white pepper
8 very thin slices lemon for garnish (optional)
4 parsley sprigs for garnish (optional)

1   Peel and finely chop enough onion to measure 60g (2 oz).
2   Combine artichoke hearts, milk, salt, sugar, and chopped onion in medium-size non-aluminium

saucepan, and simmer over medium-high heat 20 minutes. Do *not* boil.

3   Meanwhile, separate eggs into 2 small bowls, reserving whites for another use.
4   After 20 minutes, remove pan from heat and allow mixture to cool slightly.
5   Transfer mixture to food processor or blender and purée.
6   Rinse saucepan, return purée to pan, and reheat 3 minutes over medium heat; reduce heat to low, if necessary, to prevent boiling.
7   Add heavy cream to egg yolks and whisk until blended. Slowly add small amount of hot purée to cream mixture, whisking until incorporated. Then add warmed cream mixture to saucepan and stir until blended. Add freshly ground pepper to taste and heat briefly.
8   Divide soup among individual bowls and garnish each serving with 2 lemon slices and parsley sprig, if desired.

Veal Scallopini Cavour

2 tablespoons virgin olive oil
4 tablespoons unsalted butter
60 g (2 oz) plain flour
Eight 5 mm (^{1}/$_4$ inch) thick veal scallops (about 750 g (1^1/$_2$ lb) total weight), pounded 2^1/$_2$ mm (^{1}/$_8$ inch) thick
Salt and freshly ground black pepper
3 tablespoons lemon juice
100 ml (3 fl oz) dry white vermouth
1 tablespoon chopped parsley

1 Preheat oven to SLOW.
2 Combine oil and 3 tablespoons of the butter in large heavy-gauge skillet over medium-high heat.
3 Meanwhile, place flour in pie pan or on plate. Lightly dredge in flour as many scallops as will fit in skillet without crowding; shake off excess flour.
4 When butter stops foaming, add scallops to skillet and sauté about 2 minutes per side, or until browned. Sprinkle with salt and pepper to taste, transfer to platter, and place in oven. Dredge remaining scallops, sauté, and transfer to platter; return to oven.
5 Remove pan from heat and add lemon juice and vermouth, stirring to scrape up any browned bits clinging to bottom of pan.
6 Return scallops and any accumulated juices to pan, cover, and braise over low heat 25 to 30 minutes, or until tender.
7 Transfer scallops to dinner plates. Add chopped parsley and remaining butter to pan and stir until blended. Pour sauce over scallops and serve.

Peperonata

2 large red bell peppers (about 350 g (12 oz) total weight)
2 large yellow bell peppers (about 350 g (12 oz) total weight)
125 ml (4 fl oz) virgin olive oil
Salt and freshly ground black pepper

1 Wash peppers and dry. Core, halve, and remove seeds and membranes. Cut peppers lengthwise into 1 cm (¹/₂ inch) thick strips.

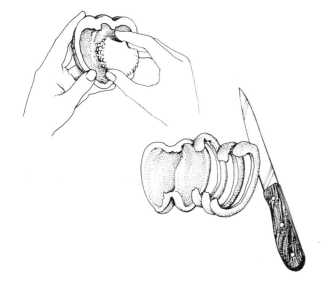

2 Heat olive oil in medium-size skillet over high heat. Add peppers and sauté, stirring, until well coated with oil, 2 to 3 minutes. Cover pan, lower heat to medium, and cook peppers 12 minutes.
3 Remove cover, add salt and pepper to taste, and cook another 10 minutes, or until pan liquid is syrupy.
4 Transfer peppers and syrup to serving dish and keep warm in SLOW oven until ready to serve.

Added touch
For this summertime dessert, use ripe freestone peaches (with easy-to-remove-remove pits) that are firm but yield slightly to pressure. To peel peaches easily, place them in boiling water for 1 minute, then immerse in cold water.

Baked Stuffed Peaches

4 large ripe freestone peaches
125 g (4 oz) granulated sugar
2 tablespoons cocoa powder
30 g (1 oz) blanched almonds, chopped
3 tablespoons grated lemon rind
5 almond macaroons (amaretti), crumbled
1 egg yolk
2 tablespoons Cognac
2 tablespoons unsalted butter

1 Preheat oven to 180°C (350°F or Mark 4).
2 Peel and halve peaches. Remove pits and discard. Using melon baller or teaspoon, scoop out all but 1 cm (¹/₂ inch) of pulp. Place pulp in medium-size mixing bowl.
3 To peach pulp, add 60 g (2 oz) sugar, cocoa, almonds, lemon rind, macaroons, egg yolk, and enough Cognac to form a thick paste, and stir to blend.
4 Arrange peach halves in shallow baking dish. Divide filling among halves, dot with butter, and sprinkle with remaining sugar. Bake peaches 20 minutes, or until a slight crust is formed on filling.
5 Divide peaches among individual plates and serve.

Leftover suggestion
Reserve the unused egg whites from the artichoke soup recipe and freeze them until you accumulate enough (about 4 to 6) to make meringues, a popular sweet in Italy. For convenience, put each white into a compartment of an ice cube tray and cover the tray tightly with foil.

Nancy Verde Barr

Menu 1
(*right*)
Braised Duck with Black Olives
Penne with Mushroom Sauce

Nancy Barr is particularly interested in recipes from southern Italy, which was her paternal grandparents' home. As a cooking teacher, her ambition is to familiarize Americans with the diversity of southern Italian food. 'I want people to know that southerners eat so many more dishes than pizza, lasagne, spaghetti, and meatballs!' she says.

Her Menus 1 and 3 introduce easy but relatively unfamiliar southern Italian dishes. In Menu 1, she serves pasta with a highly seasoned tomato sauce from the region of Calabria and couples it with braised duck and black olives from nearby Basilicata. Menu 3 features a courgette soup from Naples, lamb chops cooked with mushrooms (a dish popular in Calabria's province of Catanzaro), and broccoli rabe sautéed with olive oil and garlic.

For a change of pace, in Menu 2 Nancy Barr prepares a simple meal from the region of Abruzzo, where pickled vegetables are often cooked with chicken or veal. The tomatoes are stuffed with a mixture of bread crumbs, capers, anchovies, and *soppressata*, a hard Italian salami.

For this informal dinner, present the pieces of browned duck on a large serving platter, then spoon the olives and other sauce ingredients over the top. Penne in a spicy tomato sauce is a traditional southern Italian partner for duck.

<table>
<tr><td>Menu
1</td><td><h1>Braised Duck with Black Olives
Penne with Mushroom Sauce</h1></td></tr>
</table>

Most supermarkets sell frozen whole ducks, but because they are increasingly in demand, you can often find them fresh as well. The skin of fresh ducks should be elastic, free of pinfeathers, and should feel well padded with fat. Keep fresh duck loosely wrapped in the coldest part of the refrigerator for up to three days. Frozen ducks should be securely wrapped in sturdy, unbroken plastic wrap. They can be stored frozen for up to three months. Thaw them in the plastic wrap in the refrigerator 24 to 36 hours before cooking; or, if you are in a hurry, put the frozen duck, still wrapped in waterproof plastic, in a pan of cold water and it will be ready for cooking in about three hours.

The penne, or quill-shaped pasta, is served with a simple sauce sparked with hot pepper flakes. Start with a small amount of flakes, and adjust the seasoning to your taste. If fresh hot chilies are available, try them in place of the pepper flakes. Begin with half a small hot pepper, and increase the amount, if desired. To remove the seeds, wear rubber gloves to protect your hands. The more seeds you leave in, the hotter the flavour.

What to drink

A southern Italian red wine such as the dry and flavourful Taurasi or Aglianico del Vulture complements the strong flavours of the duck.

Start-to-Finish Steps

1 Wash parsley and fresh oregano, if using, and dry with paper towels. Chop enough parsley to measure $1/2$ cup for duck recipe and $1/4$ cup for pasta recipe; chop enough oregano to measure 2 tablespoons for pasta recipe. Peel and chop onions for duck and pasta recipes.
2 Follow duck recipe steps 1 through 6.
3 While duck is grilling follow pasta recipe steps 1 and 2.
4 Follow duck recipe step 7.
5 While duck is cooking, follow pasta recipe steps 3 through 5.
6 Follow duck recipe steps 8 and 9, and pasta recipe steps 6 through 10.
7 Follow duck recipe step 10 and pasta recipe step 11, and serve together.

Braised Duck with Black Olives

$2^1/_2$ Kg (5 lb) duckling
Small celery stalk
Small carrot
125 g (4 oz) prosciutto, unsliced
125 g (4 oz) pitted black olives
3 tablespoons olive oil
Small onion, peeled and chopped
250 ml (8 fl oz) dry white wine
30 g (1 oz) chopped parsley
1 bay leaf
Salt
Freshly ground black pepper

1 Preheat grill.
2 Remove any excess fat from cavity of duck. Trim off neck skin. Chop off wing tips and reserve with neck

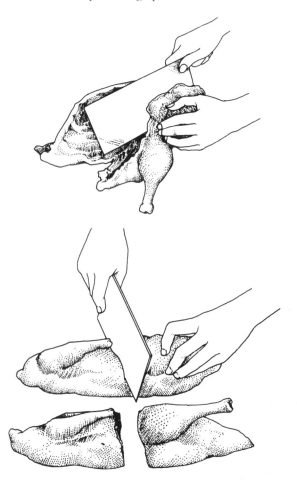

and gizzards for another use. With cleaver, quarter duck: Turn duck skin-side up on cutting surface and cut through the breastbone. Turn duck over, push back breast halves, and cut backbone in two. Next, place each half skin-side up and, feeling for end of rib cage, cut pieces in half just below ribs. Turn quarters skin-side down and, with sharp knife, trim excess skin and any visible fat from each piece.

3 Wash celery, dry, and dice enough to measure 30 g (1 oz). Peel and finely dice enough carrot to measure 30 g (1 oz). Chop prosciutto into 5 mm (1/4 inch) dice. Slice olives in half; set aside.

4 Place rack in grill pan. Place duck skin-side up on rack and grill 10 cm (6 inches) away from heating element for 5 minutes.

5 Meanwhile, heat olive oil in large sauté pan over medium heat. Add onion, celery, carrot, and prosciutto and sauté, stirring occasionally, about 10 minutes, or until onion is golden.

6 After duck has grilled 5 minutes, prick skin all over with skewer or tip of paring knife to release fat, being careful not to penetrate meat. Grill another 5 minutes, pricking skin once more during this time. Turn duck and grill another 5 minutes.

7 Transfer duck to sauté pan with vegetables and prosciutto, add wine, and bring to a boil over high heat. Reduce oven temperature to SLOW, leaving door ajar if necessary. Seal pan with sheet of foil, place cover over foil, and cook duck over medium heat 15 minutes.

8 Remove cover and foil, add parsley, bay leaves, olives, and salt and pepper to taste. Reseal pan with foil, re-cover, and cook another 20 minutes, or until tender.

9 Meanwhile, place large heatproof serving platter in oven to warm.

10 When duck is done, transfer to warm platter, top with sauce, and serve.

1 Peel and coarsely chop garlic. Wipe mushrooms clean with damp paper towels and chop coarsely.

2 In strainer set over medium-size bowl, drain tomatoes; reserve juice. Coarsely chop tomatoes; set aside.

3 Heat oil in medium-size sauté pan over medium heat. Add onion and garlic, and sauté, stirring occasionally, 3 to 4 minutes, or until onions are soft and translucent.

4 Raise heat to high, add mushrooms, and salt to taste; sauté 2 to 3 minutes, or until mushrooms exude liquid.

5 Reduce heat to medium. Add tomatoes, 125 ml (4 fl oz) reserved tomato juice, parsley, oregano, red pepper flakes, and salt to taste, and simmer 25 minutes, adding more tomato juice if sauce becomes too thick.

6 Bring 4 ltrs (6 pts) salted water to a boil in stockpot over high heat.

7 Meanwhile, in food processor or with grater, grate enough cheese to make 125 g (4 oz) and set aside.

8 Place large heatproof serving bowl in SLOW oven to warm.

9 Add penne to boiling water and cook according to package directions until *al dente*.

11 Drain pasta in colander.

12 Turn sauce into warm serving bowl, add drained pasta, and toss to combine. Serve with grated cheese.

Penne with Mushroom Sauce

Large clove garlic
350 g (12 oz) mushrooms
1 Kg (2 lb) canned Italian plum tomatoes
3 tablespoons olive oil
Small onion, peeled and chopped
salt
15 g (1/2 oz) chopped parsley
2 tablespoons chopped fresh oregano, or 2 teaspoons dried
1/4 teaspoon red pepper flakes, approximately
125 g (4 oz) pecorino Romano or Parmesan cheese
350 g (12 oz) penne or similarly shaped pasta

Menu 2

Piquant Chicken
Baked Stuffed Tomatoes

For the chicken main dish, the cook suggests butterflying a whole fryer: splitting the bird in half, removing the backbone, and opening the chicken flat. Cooking the chicken this way makes it juicier. Or, have your butcher butterfly the chicken, or substitute a cut-up fryer.

What to drink

A white Lacryma Christi or a top-quality Orvieto would be fine here, or try a California Sauvignon Blanc.

The aromas of the piquant chicken enhance this meal. Spoon some of the sauce with pickled sweet peppers and artichoke hearts over the chicken quarters, and offer a whole baked tomato with each helping.

Start-to-Finish Steps

One hour ahead: Set out artichoke hearts to thaw for chicken recipe.

1 Follow tomatoes recipe steps 1 and 2.
2 Follow chicken recipe steps 1 through 6.
3 While chicken is cooking, follow tomatoes recipe step 3.
4 Follow chicken recipe step 7 and tomatoes recipe steps 4 through 6.
5 Follow chicken recipe step 8 and tomatoes recipe steps 7 and 8.
6 Follow chicken recipe steps 9 through 12, and serve with tomatoes.

Piquant Chicken

1 frying chicken (about 1.5 Kg (3 lb))
2 large cloves garlic
4 tablespoons olive oil
125 g (4 oz) Italian pickled sweet peppers, without liquid
125 ml (4 fl oz) dry white wine
250 g (8 oz) frozen artichoke hearts, thawed
Salt

1 Rinse chicken under cold water and dry with paper towels. To butterfly chicken: Place chicken on cutting surface, breast-side down, with legs pointing toward you. Using poultry shears or chef's knife, cut along each side of backbone as close to the bone as possible. Remove backbone and discard. Turn bird breast-side up and flatten by striking breastbone with the heel of your hand. Cut off wing tips and tuck wings under.

2 Bruise garlic by placing cloves under flat blade of chef's knife; peel.

3 Heat olive oil in large skillet over medium-low heat. Add garlic and sauté, stirring occasionally, 4 to 6 minutes, or until golden. Discard garlic.

4 Place chicken skin-side down in skillet. Raise heat to medium-high and cook about 8 minutes, or until chicken skin is nicely browned.

5 Meanwhile, cut peppers into 1 cm ($^1/_2$ inch) by 5 cm (2 inch) long strips; set aside.

6 Turn chicken skin-side up and cook another 7 minutes.

7 Pour off all but 1 tablespoon fat from skillet. Add wine and bring to a boil over high heat; boil 15 seconds. Reduce heat to medium, cover, and cook 15 minutes.

8 Add pepper strips, artichoke hearts, and salt to taste to skillet. Cover and cook another 15 to 20 minutes, or until juices run clear when chicken is pierced with a sharp knife.

9 Toward end of cooking time, place 4 dinner plates under hot running water to warm.

10 When chicken is cooked, remove from pan to cutting surface. With poultry shears or chef's knife,

cut chicken into quarters. Dry plates and transfer chicken pieces to them.

11 Raise heat under skillet to high and boil pan juices, stirring to scrape up any browned bits clinging to bottom of pan, until juices are slightly thickened and glossy, 2 to 4 minutes. There should be about 60 ml (2 fl oz) of pan juices.

12 Top each serving of chicken with a spoonful of pan juices and some vegetables.

Baked Stuffed Tomatoes

4 medium-size tomatoes (about 750 g (1½ lb) total weight)
Salt
3 slices stale bread, approximately
Small bunch parsley
125 g (4 oz) jar capers
2 to 4 anchovy fillets
125 g (4 oz) soppressata or other hard salami
3 tablespoons olive oil, approximately
Freshly ground black pepper

1 Preheat oven to 190°C (375°F or Mark 5).

2 Cut 1 cm (½ inch) slice from tops of tomatoes. Turn each tomato upside down and squeeze gently to remove seeds and juice. Using serrated or regular teaspoon, remove any remaining seeds and enough pulp to make room for stuffing. Sprinkle insides of tomatoes lightly with salt and place upside down on paper-towel-covered cake rack to drain.

3 Trim off crusts from bread and discard. Using food processor or grater, grate enough bread to measure 60 g (2 oz) crumbs.

4 Rinse parsley and dry with paper towels; finely chop enough to measure 15 g (½ oz). Drain 1 tablespoon capers in small strainer and rinse under cold running water; chop finely. Drain anchovies; chop finely. Finely chop soppressata.

5 Combine parsley, capers, anchovies, soppressata, and bread crumbs in small bowl. Add 1 tablespoon olive oil to mixture and stir until blended. Add pepper to taste but *no* salt; the capers and anchovies provide sufficient saltiness.

6 Divide stuffing among tomato shells.

7 Lightly grease shallow baking dish with some of the remaining oil. Place tomatoes upright in dish and drizzle with 1 or 2 teaspoons olive oil.

8 Bake 20 minutes, or until tomatoes are lightly browned on top.

Added touch
Pumate, or dried Italian plum tomatoes, are used in this pasta dish – here in their oil-packed form. They are used sparingly because their concentrated tomato flavour can be overpowering. The richly flavoured oil makes a good seasoning for salad dressings or garlic bread.

Linguine with Onions

3 medium-size onions (about 350 g (12 oz) total weight)
125 ml (4 fl oz) plus 3 tablespoons olive oil
2 tablespoons fresh oregano, preferably, or other fresh herb such as marjoram or parsley
125 g (4 oz) jar sun-dried tomatoes in olive oil
125 g (4 oz) Kalamata olives
3 slices bread
Salt and freshly ground black pepper
350 g (12 oz) linguine, preferably imported

1 Peel and halve onions, then cut crosswise into thin semicircles.

2 Heat 125 ml (4 fl oz) oil in medium-size sauté pan over medium-low heat. Add onions, cover, and cook until completely softened, about 30 minutes. Do *not* allow onions to brown.

3 Meanwhile, wash fresh oregano and pat dry with paper towels. Coarsely chop enough oregano to measure 2 tablespoons. Cut sun-dried tomatoes into 5 mm (¼ inch) wide strips. Pit olives and cut lengthwise into quarters.

4 Trim off crusts from bread and discard. In food processor or with grater, grate enough bread to measure 100 g (3 oz) crumbs.

5 When olives are ready, stir in oregano, tomatoes, olives, and salt and freshly ground pepper to taste, and cook gently, uncovered, 10 minutes.

6 Meanwhile, in stockpot, bring 4 ltrs (6 pts) salted water to a boil over high heat.

7 Heat remaining 3 tablespoons olive oil in small skillet over high heat. Add bread crumbs and toss with fork until golden and toasted, about 4 minutes. Set aside.

8 Transfer onion mixture to large serving bowl.

9 Add linguine to boiling water and cook according to package directions until *al dente.*

10 Drain linguine in colander, turn into bowl with onion mixture, and toss to combine. Sprinkle with toasted bread crumbs and serve.

Courgette Soup
Lamb Catanzaro-style
Broccoli Rabe

The courgette soup can precede the main course of broccoli rabe and lamb chops topped with mushrooms and onions.

49

Whole beaten eggs thicken the courgette soup. To prevent the eggs from coagulating, first add a small portion of soup to the beaten eggs, stirring continuously. Then blend the warmed eggs into the soup. If the eggs scramble slightly despite this measure, the flavour of the soup will not be affected.

Two two-step cooking technique for the broccoli rabe is used throughout Italy. Blanching the vegetable before sautéing it eliminates any bitterness. You may substitute turnip, beet, or mustard greens, but cooking times for these greens vary, so check for doneness.

What to drink
A light red wine would best suit this menu. Choose a young Chianti, Valpolicella, or Bardolino, or a domestic Beaujolais-style Zinfandel.

Start-to-Finish Steps
1   Follow soup recipe steps 1 through 10.
2   Follow lamb recipe steps 1 through 6.
3   Follow broccoli rabe recipe steps 1 and 2.
4   Follow lamb recipe steps 7 and 8.
5   Follow broccoli rabe recipe steps 3 through 6.
6   Follow lamb recipe step 9 and broccoli rabe recipe step 7.
7   While broccoli rabe cooks, follow soup recipe steps 11 and 12, and serve.
8   Follow lamb recipe steps 10 through 12 and broccoli rabe recipe step 8, and serve.

Courgette Soup

Small bunch fresh parsley
Small bunch fresh oregano, or 2 teaspoons dried
4 medium-size courgettes (about 825 g (1¾ lb) total weight)
Medium-size onion (about 250 g (8 oz))
60 g (2 oz) pecorino Romano or Parmesan cheese
Four 2 cm (¾ inch) thick slices Italian bread
2 tablespoons lard
2 tablespoons olive oil
1 lltr (1¾ pts) beef stock
Salt
Freshly ground black pepper
2 large eggs

1   Preheat oven to 180°C (350°F or Mark 4).
2   Wash parsley and fresh oregano and dry with paper towels. Chop enough parsley to measure 15 g (½ oz). Chop enough oregano to measure 2 tablespoons. Wash courgettes, dry, and trim off ends. Cut courgettes into 1 cm (½ inch) slices. Peel and slice onion crosswise into thin rounds.
3   In food processor or with grater, grate enough cheese to measure 60 g (2 oz); set aside.
4   Arrange bread in single layer on baking sheet and toast in oven 5 minutes.
5   While bread is toasting, combine lard and olive oil in large heavy-gauge saucepan over medium heat. Add onion and sauté, stirring occasionally, 4 to 5 minutes, or until soft and translucent.
6   Turn bread and toast on other side another 5 minutes.
7   Meanwhile, bring stock to a gentle simmer in small saucepan over medium heat.
8   Add courgettes to onion and toss to combine. Add hot stock and salt and pepper to taste, and simmer gently 15 to 20 minutes, or until courgettes are tender.
9   Meanwhile, remove bread from oven and set aside. Reduce oven temperature to SLOW.
10 In medium-size bowl, combine eggs, grated cheese, and chopped herbs, and beat until blended; set aside.
11 Beating continuously with wooden spoon, slowly add 250 ml (8 fl oz) of hot soup to egg mixture; then gradually add egg mixture to soup, stirring continuously until blended. Heat soup just to a simmer; do *not* boil.
12 Place a slice of toasted bread in each of 4 soup bowls. Divide soup among bowls, and serve.

Lamb Catanzaro-style

Medium-size onion (about 250 g (8 oz))
250 g (8 oz) mushrooms
125 g (4 oz) jar capers
60 g (2 oz) anchovy fillets
125 ml (4 fl oz) plus 3 tablespoons olive oil
30 g (1 oz) plain flour, approximately
Eight 2 cm (3/4 inch) thick rib lamb chops (about
    1.25 Kg (2 1/2 lb) total weight)
Salt
Freshly ground black pepper
125 ml (4 fl oz) dry white wine

1 Peel and finely chop enough onion to
   measure 30 g (1 oz). Wipe mushrooms clean
   with damp paper towels and cut into 2 1/2 mm
   (1/8 inch) slices.
2 Rinse 2 tablespoons capers in small strainer under
   cold running water and drain. Rinse 3 anchovy
   fillets under cold running water and dry with
   paper towels. Coarsely chop capers and anchovies.
3 Heat 3 tablespoons olive oil in medium-size non-
   aluminium skillet over medium heat. Add onion
   and sauté, stirring occasionally, 5 to 8 minutes, or
   until onion is golden.
4 Meanwhile, place flour in pie pan or flat shallow
   dish. Trim off excess fat from lamb chops and dust
   chops lightly with flour.
5 Heat remaining olive oil in large heavy-gauge
   skillet over medium-high heat. Add chops and
   brown 5 to 6 minutes on one side.
6 While chops are cooking, add mushrooms, and
   salt and pepper to taste to onions, and sauté,
   stirring occasionally, 3 to 5 minutes, or until
   mushrooms release their juices.
7 Using metal tongs, turn chops and brown on other
   side another 5 to 6 minutes.
8 Cover onion-mushroom mixture, remove pan from
   heat, and set aside.
9 With slotted metal spatula, transfer chops to
   heatproof platter, sprinkle with salt and pepper,
   and place in SLOW oven.
10 Pour off all but 2 tablespoons of fat from skillet.
   Return skillet to high heat, add wine and any juices
   that have accumulated around lamb chops, and
   bring to a boil, scraping up any browned bits
   clinging to bottom of pan. Continue boiling 2 to 3
   minutes, or until liquid is reduced by half.
11 Add reduced pan juices to onion-mushroom
   mixture and stir to combine. Reheat briefly over
   medium heat.
12 Divide lamb chops among 4 dinner plates and top
   each serving with some of the onion-mushroom
   mixture.

Broccoli Rabe

Salt
750 g (1 1/2 lb) broccoli rabe or turnip, beet, or
    mustard greens
2 medium-size cloves garlic
2 lemons
4 tablespoons olive oil
Freshly ground black pepper

1 Bring 2 1/2 ltrs (4 pts) of lightly salted water to a boil
   in stockpot over high heat.
2 Meanwhile, remove tough outer leaves from
   broccoli rabe and discard. With paring knife, peel
   stems and wash broccoli rabe thoroughly under
   cold running water. Cut each stalk into thirds.

Broccoli rabe

3 Add broccoli rabe to boiling water and cook 3
   minutes.
4 While broccoli rabe is cooking, bruise garlic under
   flat blade of chef's knife and peel. Rinse 1 lemon,
   dry, and cut into 8 wedges; set aside. Halve
   remaining lemon. Squeeze juice of one half and set
   aside; reserve other half for another use.
5 Turn broccoli rabe into colander, refresh under
   cold running water, and drain. Wrap in clean
   kitchen towel or paper towels to dry.
6 Heat olive oil in large sauté pan over medium heat.
   Add garlic and sauté 2 to 3 minutes, or until lightly
   golden.
7 Add broccoli rabe, and salt and pepper to taste,
   cover pan, and cook 10 to 12 minutes, or until
   broccoli rabe is fork-tender.
8 Remove garlic and discard. Sprinkle broccoli rabe
   with lemon juice, divide among 4 dinner plates,
   and serve with lemon wedges.

Robert Pucci

Menu 1
(*right*)
Braised Beef Tenderloin in Wine Sauce
Potatoes Parmigiana
Sautéed Vegetables

Properly prepared Italian food is particularly wholesome and often low in fat, qualities that Robert Pucci's three menus highlight. For Menu 1, an adaptation of a restaurant meal he had in Rome, he serves an entrée of braised tenderloin steaks, mashed potatoes flavoured with grated Parmesan cheese, and a mix of fresh vegetables. Although in Italy carbohydrates are rarely eaten with the main course, mashed potatoes with braised meat are an exception.

Menu 2, an amalgam of many striking Italian flavours, begins with a Venetian-style linguine that combines freshly grated Parmesan cheese with baby clams. Flounder fillets in a zesty tomato sauce with capers and black olives (the recipe is named for Sorrento, a town near Naples) and Ligurian spinach, pine nuts, and raisins are presented after the pasta.

Well-balanced in taste, texture, and colour, Menu 3 can be planned with the angel hair pasta as the first course, followed by veal Marsala and a salad of steamed vegetables marinated in a garlic and basil vinaigrette. Or serve the salad as the appetizer and the pasta and veal together.

For an elegant dinner for company, serve individual tenderloin steaks with a creamy wine sauce, sautéed vegetables, and mashed potatoes with Parmesan and parsley.

53

Braised Beef Tenderloin in Wine Sauce
Potatoes Parmigiana
Sautéed Vegetables

Beef tenderloin steaks are served here with a cream-enriched Marsala and red wine sauce. Dry Marsalas are preferable for red meat dishes.

For the fluffiest mashed potatoes, use a high-starch potato variety such as russet. Long ovals with rough surfaces, russets – like all potatoes – should be clean, firm, and smooth without wilt, soft dark spots, a green tinge, or sprouts. Never store potatoes in the refrigerator because cold temperatures convert the starch into sugar, making the potatoes too sweet.

What to drink
The cook suggests a full-bodied Chianti Classico to complement this menu; a Spanna or Nebbiolo is also fine.

Start-to-Finish Steps

Thirty minutes ahead: Set out 125 ml (4 fl oz) heavy cream to bring to room temperature for potatoes recipe.

1 Peel and mince garlic for beef and vegetables recipes; peel garlic clove for potatoes recipe.
2 Follow potatoes recipe steps 1 through 5.
3 Follow vegetables recipe steps 1 and 2.
4 Follow potatoes recipe steps 6 through 9.
5 Follow vegetables recipe steps 3 through 7.
6 Follow beef recipe steps 1 through 9.
7 Follow vegetables recipe steps 8 through 10.
8 Follow beef recipe steps 10 through 12, potatoes recipe step 10, and serve with vegetables.

125 ml (4 fl oz) full-bodied dry red wine, such as Chianti
125 ml (4 fl oz) heavy cream, approximately

1 Preheat oven to SLOW.
2 Crush fennel seeds between 2 sheets of waxed paper with rolling pin.
3 Combine butter and oil in medium-size heavy-gauge skillet over high heat. Add steaks and cook 2 to 3 minutes per side, or until brown.
4 Using tongs, transfer steaks to platter and salt lightly. Cover loosely with foil to keep warm and set aside.
5 Reduce heat under skillet to medium-low. Stir in garlic, red pepper flakes, and crushed fennel, and cook 1 minute.
6 Add tomato paste; cook, stirring, another 2 minutes.
7 Increase heat to medium, add Marsala and red wine, and cook about 5 minutes, or until reduced by half.
8 Place 4 dinner plates in oven to warm.
9 Reduce heat under skillet to low, stir in heavy cream to taste, and cook about 5 minutes, or until sauce is thick enough to coat back of spoon.
10 Strain sauce into small bowl and return to skillet.
11 Stir in any juices that have accumulated on platter with steaks and return steaks to skillet. Over low heat, reheat steaks about 2 minutes, turning one to coat with sauce. If sauce separates, whisk in a bit more cream.
12 Place 1 steak on each dinner plate and top with sauce.

Braised Beef Tenderloin in Wine Sauce

1 tablespoon fennel seeds
2 tablespoons unsalted butter
2 tablespoons virgin olive oil
Four 2½ cm (1 inch) thick beef tenderloin steaks (about 625–750 g (1¼–1½ lb) total weight)
Salt
2 teaspoons finely minced garlic
½ teaspoon red pepper flakes
1 tablespoon tomato paste
125 ml (4 fl oz) dry Marsala, preferably Florio or Rallo

Potatoes Parmigiana

Large clove garlic, peeled
Salt
1 Kg (2 lb) boiling potatoes
Small bunch parsley
60 g (2 oz) Parmesan cheese, preferably imported
125 ml (4 fl oz) heavy cream, at room temperature
¼ teaspoon freshly grated nutmeg
Freshly ground black pepper

1 Crush garlic under flat blade of chef's knife.
2 Bring 2½ ltrs (4 pts) water, ½ teaspoon salt, and

crushed garlic to a boil in large saucepan over medium-high heat.

3   Fill large bowl half full with cold water. Peel potatoes, placing in bowl of water; cut into 2½ cm (1 inch) chunks.

4   Add potatoes to boiling water and cook 15 to 20 minutes, or until tender when pierced with a sharp knife.

5   Meanwhile, rinse parsley, dry with paper towels, and chop enough to measure 2 tablespoons. Using grater, grate cheese to measure 60 g (2 oz). Place 1 tablespoon parsley and all of the grated cheese in small bowl and toss with fork; set aside. Reserve remaining chopped parsley.

6   Drain potatoes, reserving 125 ml (4 fl oz) cooking water. Transfer potatoes to large heatproof bowl.

7   With electric mixer, beat potatoes until smooth, adding a bit reserved cooking water if they seem dry.

8   Add cream, nutmeg, and salt and pepper to taste, and beat until blended.

9   Add Parmesan and parsley and beat to combine. Adjust seasoning, cover potatoes loosely with foil, and keep warm in SLOW oven until ready to serve.

10 Divide mashed potatoes among dinner plates, sprinkle with reserved parsley, and serve.

Sautéed Vegetables

250 g (8 oz) carrots
250 g (8 oz) asparagus, if available, or snow peas
125 g (4 oz) summer squash, if available
125 g (4 oz) very small courgettes, or 250 g (8 oz), if not using summer squash
1 yellow bell pepper
1 red bell pepper
Small onion
3 tablespoons unsalted butter
3 tablespoons olive oil
Large clove garlic, finely minced
1 lemon
Salt and freshly ground black pepper

1   Wash vegetables and dry with paper towels. Peel carrots and cut into 3½ cm (1½ inch) pieces. Halve pieces lengthwise and cut into 5 mm (¼ inch) thick julienne. Break off tough bottom ends of asparagus and peel, if desired. Trim off ends of summer squash and courgettes, and discard. Cut crosswise into 3½ cm (1½ inch) long pieces. Halve pieces lengthwise. Remove seeds with teaspoon and discard. Cut summer squash and courgettes into 5 mm (¼ inch) thick julienne. Halve, core, and seed bell peppers. Cut into 5 mm (¼ inch) strips. Peel and quarter onion; cut lengthwise into 2½ mm (⅛ inch) slivers.

2   In medium-size saucepan fitted with vegetable steamer, bring to a boil enough water to come just up to but not above bottom of steamer.

3   Add carrots and steam 1½ to 2 minutes, or until crisp-tender. Transfer carrots to colander, refresh under cold running water, and drain.

4   Add asparagus to pan and steam 2 to 3 minutes.

5   Transfer cooked carrots to plate and set aside.

6   Transfer asparagus to colander, refresh under cold running water, and drain.

7   Add summer squash and courgettes to pan and steam 1 minute. Transfer to colander, refresh under cold running water, and drain.

8   Combine butter and oil in large heavy-gauge skillet over medium heat. Add onion and sauté, stirring, 2 minutes. The add garlic and sauté 1 minute.

9   One at a time, add vegetables, stirring after each addition to combine, and cook 2 to 3 minutes, or just until vegetables are heated through.

10 Meanwhile, squeeze enough lemon juice to measure 1 tablespoon. Add lemon juice and salt and pepper to taste to vegetables. Turn vegetables into heatproof casserole, cover loosely with foil, and keep warm in SLOW oven until ready to serve.

Linguine with Clam Sauce
Fillets of Flounder Sorrento
Sautéed Spinach with Pine Nuts and Raisins

Baked flounder fillets in a sauce of onions, black olives, and tomatoes are accompanied by sautéed spinach with pine nuts and raisins. Mixing white and green linguine gives the pasta dish greater visual appeal.

Flounder has tender, white flesh and a delicate flavour. Select firm moist fillets with a fresh aroma, and refrigerate them well-wrapped until ready to use. To prevent sticking, coat the baking dish with sauce before adding the fish. Baking the fillets briefly keeps them from toughening. Cod, sole, or halibut are also good in this recipe.

What to drink

A crisp, dry white wine such as Verdicchio is the best choice here. Greco di Tufo and white Lacryma Christi are suitable options, as is a good French Chablis.

Start-to-Finish Steps

1   Peel and mince garlic for linguine, fish, and spinach recipes. Grate Parmesan for linguine and spinach recipes.
2   Follow fish recipe steps 1 and 2, and spinach recipe steps 1 and 2.
3   Follow fish recipe steps 3 through 5.
4   Follow spinach recipe step 3 and linguine recipe steps 1 through 5.
5   While sauce is simmering, follow fish recipe step 6.
6   Follow linguine recipe steps 6 and 7, and fish recipe step 7.
7   Follow linguine recipe step 8 and serve as first course.
8   Follow fish recipe steps 8 through 10.
9   While fish is baking, follow spinach recipe steps 4 through 6.
10 Follow fish recipe steps 11 and 12.
11 Follow spinach recipe steps 7 through 9, fish recipe step 13, and serve.

Linguine with Clam Sauce

Small bunch fresh parsley
2 tablespoons capers
Salt
2 tablespoons olive oil
4 tablespoons unsalted butter, approximately
1 1/2 teaspoons minced garlic
300 g (10 oz) canned whole baby clams
100 ml (3 fl oz) dry white wine
350 g (12 fl oz) white and green linguine combined
60 g (2 oz) freshly grated Parmesan cheese
Freshly ground black pepper

1. Wash parsley and dry with paper towels. Chop enough to measure 4 tablespoons; reserve remainder for another use. Drain capers and chop, if large; set aside.
2. Bring $2^{1}/_{2}$ ltrs (4 pts) salted water to a boil in stockpot over medium-high heat.
3. Meanwhile, combine oil and 2 tablespoons butter in large skillet over low heat. Add garlic and sauté 2 minutes.
4. Add 2 tablespoons parsley to skillet; sauté 30 seconds.
5. Strain canned clam broth into skillet; reserve clams. Stir in white wine and simmer, uncovered, 10 to 15 minutes, or until thick.
6. Add linguine to boiling water and cook 8 to 10 minutes, or according to package directions for desired doneness.
7. Add capers and clams to sauce, and simmer about 2 minutes, or just until heated through.
8. Turn pasta into colander and drain. Add pasta to sauce in skillet and toss to combine. Add Parmesan, remaining parsley, 1 or 2 tablespoons of remaining butter, and pepper to taste, and toss. Turn into large bowl and serve.

Fillets of Flounder Sorrento

Small bunch fresh oregano, or 1 teaspoon dried
Large onion
250 g (8 oz) canned Italian plum tomatoes
2 tablespoons capers
3 tablespoons olive oil
2 teaspoons minced garlic
Salt and freshly ground black pepper
30 g (1 oz) oil-cured black olives
4 fillets of flounder (625 –750 g (1–1$^{1}/_{4}$ lb) total weight)
125 g (4 fl oz) dry white wine

1. If using fresh oregano, wash and dry with paper towels. Chop enough to measure 1 tablespoon, reserving remainder for another use. Peel and thinly slice onion. Drain tomatoes, reserving juice for another use, and chop enough to measure 175 g (6 oz). Drain capers.
2. Heat olive oil in medium-size skillet over medium heat. Add onion and sauté, stirring occasionally, about 8 minutes, or until golden.
3. Add garlic and sauté 1 minute.
4. Add tomatoes, oregano, and salt and pepper to taste, reduce heat to medium-low, and simmer about 15 minutes, or until sauce is thickened.
5. Meanwhile, preheat oven to 230°C (450°F or Mark 8).

6. Pit olives and chop coarsely. Add olives and capers to sauce and simmer another 5 minutes.
7. Remove pan from heat, cover, and set aside.
8. Wash fillets and dry with paper towels.
9. Coat baking dish with spoonful of sauce. One at a time, arrange fillets in dish: Top each with a spoonful of sauce and then overlap with another fillet. Pour wine over fish and bake 6 to 8 minutes, or until fish flakes easily when tested with fork.
10. Place serving platter under hot water to warm.
11. When fish is done, dry platter. With wide metal spatula, gently transfer fillets with sauce to warm platter.
12. Strain pan juices into small saucepan; reduce over high heat 2 to 3 minutes, or until slightly thickened.
13. Pour reduced pan juices over fillets and serve.

Sautéed Spinach with Pine Nuts and Raisins

750 g (1$^{1}/_{2}$ lb) spinach
4 tablespoons unsalted butter
1 teaspoon minced garlic
2 rolled anchovies
2 tablespoons pine nuts
$^{1}/_{4}$ teaspoon freshly grated nutmeg
Salt and freshly ground black pepper
2 tablespoons golden raisins
2 tablespoons freshly grated Parmesan cheese

1. Remove stems from spinach and discard. Wash spinach thoroughly in several changes of cold water; do *not* dry.
2. Add spinach to stockpot and cook over medium-low heat about 5 minutes, or until wilted.
3. Turn spinach into colander, cool under cold running water, and press out excess water with back of spoon. Chop spinach coarsely; set aside.
4. Heat butter in medium-size sauté pan over low heat. Add garlic and sauté about 1 minute.
5. Add anchovies and mash into butter with back of spoon.
6. Add spinach and sauté over low heat, stirring occasionally, 5 minutes, or until moisture has evaporated. Place serving bowl under hot running water to warm.
7. Add pine nuts and nutmeg to spinach, and salt and pepper to taste; stir to combine.
8. Add raisins to mixture and continue cooking just until raisins are heated through, about 1 minute.
9. Dry serving bowl. Add Parmesan to spinach, stir to combine, and turn into warm bowl.

<table>
<tr><td>

</td><td>

Angel Hair Pasta with Onions and Pepper Strips
Veal Scallopini Marsala
Warm Vegetable Salad

</td></tr>
</table>

Veal scallops subtly flavoured with Marsala and a warm vegetable salad complement a bowl of angel hair pasta.

Veal scallopini, or scallops, are thin slices cut from the leg, which are pounded to flatten them for quick and uniform cooking. Remove any fat or filament before sprinkling the veal with flour. Scallops are best fried or sautéed briefly over medium heat so that they cook through quickly. You can also use scallops of turkey.

What to drink

Try a firm, somewhat fruity white wine, such as an Italian Chardonnay or a Tocai from Friuli.

Start-to-Finish Steps

1   Wash parsley and fresh basil, if using, and dry with paper towels. Chop enough parsley to measure 2 tablespoons for veal recipe and 2 tablespoons for pasta recipe. Chop enough basil to measure 3 tablespoons for salad recipe and refrigerate remainder for another use.
2   Follow pasta recipe steps 1 through 4.
3   Follow salad recipe steps 1 through 4.
4   Follow veal recipe steps 1 through 4.
5   Follow salad recipe step 5.
6   Follow pasta recipe steps 5 through 9, and serve as first course.
7   Follow veal recipe step 5 and salad recipe step 6.
8   Follow veal recipe step 6 and salad recipe step 7.
9   Follow veal recipe steps 7 and 8, and serve with salad.

Angel Hair Pasta with Onions and Pepper Strips

1 lemon
Small red onion
500 g (1 lb) white or yellow onions
4 tablespoons olive oil, preferably imported
3/4 teaspoon salt
1/4 teaspoon freshly ground black pepper
Pinch of sugar
1 red bell pepper
60 g (2 oz) Parmesan cheese
250 g (8 oz) angel hair pasta (capelli d'angelo) or capellini
2 to 4 tablespoons unsalted butter
2 tablespoons chopped fresh parsley

1   Wash lemon, dry, and cut in half lengthwise. With paring knife, remove peel from one half of lemon, avoiding white pith; reserve remaining half for another use.
2   Peel red onion; cut into thin slices, separate into rings, and set aside. Peel and quarter white or yellow onions; cut into thin slivers. You will have about 60 g (2 oz) red onion and about 250 g (8 oz) white or yellow onions.
3   Heat oil in heatproof casserole over low heat. Add lemon peel and sauté 2 minutes.
4   Stir in slivered onions, salt, pepper, and pinch of sugar. Raise heat to medium, cover the casserole, and simmer, stirring occasionally to prevent sticking, 20 to 30 minutes, or until onions are well browned.
5   Bring 4 ltrs (6 pts) of water to a boil over high heat.
6   Wash and dry red bell pepper. Halve, core, and seed pepper, and cut into 2 1/2 mm (1/8 inch) thick strips. Set aside. Grate Parmesan to measure 60 g (2 oz). Set aside.
7   Add pasta to boiling water and, after water returns to a boil, cook about 30 seconds for angel hair pasta or 2 to 3 minutes for capellini. Turn pasta into colander to drain.
8   Add pasta to onions in casserole and toss gently.
9   Add red onion rings, pepper strips, butter to taste, parsley, and 30 g (1 oz) grated Parmesan to pasta, and toss. Divide pasta among bowls and serve with remaining Parmesan.

Veal Scallopini Marsala

2 tablespoons vegetable oil or light olive oil
30 g (1 oz) plain flour, approximately
8 veal scallops (about 625 g (1 1/4 lb) total weight), pounded 5 mm (1/4 inch) thick
4 tablespoons unsalted butter
125 ml (4 fl oz) sweet Marsala
2 tablespoons chopped parsley

1   Preheat oven to SLOW.
2   Heat oil in large heavy-gauge skillet over medium-high heat.
3   Meanwhile, place flour in pie pan or shallow dish. One by one, dust each scallop very lightly with flour, place in skillet, and sauté about 1 minute per side. Do *not* over-crowd skillet; cook scallops in 2 batches, if necessary.
4   As they are cooked, transfer scallops to heatproof platter and keep warm in oven; wipe out skillet.
5   Place 4 dinner plates in oven to warm.
6   Add butter and Marsala to skillet and bring to a boil over high heat; continue boiling 2 to 3 minutes, or until slightly thickened.
7   Reduce heat to low. Return scallops to pan and, using tongs, turn scallops several times until well coated.
8   Divide scallops among warm plates and sprinkle each serving with parsley.

Warm Vegetable Sauce

300 g (10 oz) cherry tomatoes
250 g (8 oz) summer squash, if available
250 g (8 oz) courgettes, or 500 g (1 lb), if not using summer squash
250 g (8 oz) carrots
Large clove garlic
125 ml (4 fl oz) olive oil, preferably imported
2 to 3 tablespoons chopped fresh basil, or 2 to 3 teaspoons dried
Pinch sugar
1 teaspoon salt
$^1/_2$ teaspoon freshly ground black pepper
2 tablespoons red wine vinegar, preferably imported

1. In medium-size saucepan fitted with vegetable steamer, bring to a boil enough water to come just up to but not above bottom of steamer.
2. Meanwhile, wash and dry tomatoes. Wash summer squash, and courgettes and discard tops and tails. Cut into 2 cm ($^3/_4$ inch) rounds. Peel carrots, Cut into $3^1/_2$ cm ($1^1/_2$ inch) long pieces, and cut each piece lengthwise into quarters.
3. Place squash and courgettes in steamer; steam 2 minutes.
4. Transfer squash to large heatproof bowl. Place carrots in steamer and steam 10 minutes.
5. Add carrots to squash, cover and keep warm in oven.
6. Combine oil, basil, pinch of sugar, salt, and pepper in small saucepan. Put garlic through press, add to mixture in pan, and cook over low heat for 4 minutes.
7. Stir in vinegar and pour warm dressing over vegetables. Add whole cherry tomatoes and toss to combine.

Added touch

For this creamy ricotta pudding, use imported Italian candied citrus peel if possible. If peel is unavailable, increase the mixture of dark and golden raisins and currants proportionately.

Ricotta Pudding

2 tablespoons candied citrus peel
1 tablespoon dark raisins
1 tablespoon golden raisins
1 tablespoon currants
60 ml (2 fl oz) brandy or fruit-flavored liqueur
4 large eggs, at room temperature, separated
100 g (3 oz) granulated sugar
750 g ($1^1/_2$ lb) ricotta or cottage cheese
Grated peel of 1 lemon
$^1/_2$ teaspoon vanilla extract
2 tablespoons all-purpose flour
Salt
1 tablespoon unsalted butter, approximately
30 g (1 oz) dried bread crumbs, approximately
Confectioners' sugar

1. Preheat oven to 180°C (350°F or Mark 4).
2. Chop candied citrus peel and combine with raisins, and currants, and brandy in a small bowl. Set aside to soak at least 15 minutes.
3. If using food processor, combine egg yolks, sugar, cheese, lemon peel, and vanilla, and process until combined. Add flour and process until blended. If using electric mixer, first combine yolks and sugar, and beat until thoroughly blended before adding cheese, flavourings, and flour.
4. Add brandy but not fruit to the mixture and blend; then add the fruit and blend briefly to combine.
5. Beat egg whites with a pinch of salt until stiff. Pour one third of cheese mixture over egg whites and gently fold in until totally incorporated.
6. Generously butter $1^1/_2$ ltr (3 pt) soufflé dish. Add bread crumbs and evenly coat dish.
7. Turn pudding into prepared dish and place in baking pan. Fill pan with enough hot water to come halfway up sides of soufflé dish and bake 60 to 70 minutes, or until pudding is nicely browned.
8. Remove pudding from oven and let stand in water bath 30 minutes before unmoulding.
9. To unmould, run thin-bladed knife around edge of soufflé dish. Place large flat plate upside down over dish and, holding plate and dish firmly together, turn upside down. If pudding does not unmould, rap plate and dish once against hard surface. Remove soufflé dish.
10. Sprinkle pudding with confectioners' sugar and serve.

Meet the Cooks

Silvana La Rocca

The daughter of an Italian diplomat, Silvana La Rocca was born and raised in the Abruzzo region of central Italy. Although she holds a Master's Degree in international law, Silvana La Rocca cooks for a living. She resides in California, where she operates a delicatessen, take-out and catering business.

Felice and Lidia Bastianich

Felice Bastianich and his wife, Lidia, were born in Istria, but met and married in New York. They opened their first restaurant in Queens in 1970 and now own and operate Felidia in Manhattan, which features authentic Italian regional food with a focus on Istrian dishes.

Lynne Kasper

Cooking teacher and food writer Lynne Kasper has studied with many leading cooks and at L'Ecole de Cuisine La Varenne in Paris. She is a founding member of the International Association of Cooking Schools and a regular contributor to magazines. She now lives in Brussels where she teaches cookery.

Susan DeRege

Born in Ontario, Canada, Susan DeRege is married to a native of Piedmont, Italy. She has travelled throughout northern Italy gathering unusual and authentic recipes and has worked as a test-kitchen home economist.

Nancy Verde Barr

A specialist in southern Italian cookery, Nancy Barr studied at Modern Gourmet in Massachusetts. She has taught cooking in France and at the Chefs Company Cooking School in Rhode Island.

Robert Pucci

Robert Pucci lives in Austin, Texas, and runs Pasta by Pucci, a catering business that specializes in Italian cooking. Besides catering, he works as a cook for several families. Interested in food since childhood, he lived in Italy for a year, studying and sampling the country's regional dishes.

A Wealth of Herbs

Increasingly, herbs are arriving in the markets fresh; the proliferation of health stores and other specialist shops has widened choice, and many cooks with gardens have taken to raising their own. Recent ethnic influences have called attention to once seemingly esoteric herbs. Coriander, for one, is at last gaining deserved popularity in Europe, although cooks in Asia and the Middle East have been using it for centuries.

Anyone wishing to dry fresh herbs can tie them loosely in a bundle and hang them upside down in a cool, dark, well-ventilated place for several weeks. When the leaves are completely dried, strip them from the stems and store them in an airtight container.

Two swifter methods of preserving herbs make use of the microwave oven and the freezer. To microwave herbs, place five or six sprigs at a time between paper towels and microwave them on high for 1 to 3 minutes until the leaves are brittle. Store the leaves loosely in airtight jars.

To freeze herbs, rinse the sprigs and pat them dry. Strip the leaves off the stems and put them into a heavy-duty plastic bag. Gently flatten the bag to force out the air, seal the bag tightly, and place it in your freezer. Use the leaves as the need arises.

Basil (also called sweet basil): This fragrant herb, with its underlying flavour of anise and hint of clove, goes particularly well with tomato.

Chervil: The small, lacy leaves of this herb have a taste akin to parsley with a touch of anise. It is good in salads and salad dressings. Chervil is popular in France where it is often an ingredient in herb mixtures, including *fines herbes*. When used in cooking, chervil should be added at the end, lest its subtle flavour be lost.

Chives: The smallest of the onions, chives grow in grassy clumps. When finely cut, the hollow leaves contribute their delicate, oniony flavour to fresh salads and raw vegetables. Chives should always be used fresh, as dried ones are virtually tasteless.

Coriander (also called cilantro): The serrated leaves of the coriander plant impart a distinctive fragrance and a flavour that is both mildly sweet and bitter. Coriander leaves should be used fresh or added at the end of cooking if their flavour is to be appreciated fully.

Dill: A sprightly herb with feathery leaves, dill enhances cucumber and many other fresh vegetables, as well as fish and shellfish. When used in cooking, dill should be added towards the end of the process to preserve its delicate flavour. Both dill seeds and dill leaves can be

What a Wedding!

New Wedding Planning,
Ideas, and Inspiration

gestalten

Table of Contents

Table of Contents

*

What a Wedding! Your Big Day, Your Way

Gorgeous ideas from 23 joyous,
offbeat, and inspiring weddings from
all over the world

First things first: give each other a smooch, pop the Champagne, and twirl around your living room. You're engaged! Congratulations! You have some exciting months of planning and anticipation ahead of your big day. Of course, smart couples don't try to do it all themselves; they get help. After all, the best weddings are those that have been planned with precision. The following pages are packed with inspiration, expert knowledge, and tips that you can draw upon to create your very own dream wedding. From an intimate beach ceremony in Portugal and a wedding in a circus tent to a DIY garden party, a Caribbean elopement, and a *grand* celebration in an opulent hacienda, *What a Wedding!* gives you a glimpse of weddings all over the world and introduces you to couples who have made their ideas for the ceremony, venue, and party a reality—and a roaring success.

> "The oufits become a statement about who they are, while the celebration symbolizes the lifestyle that they've chosen together."

Some of these weddings couldn't be more different, but what unites them is the love that the couples share. These brides and grooms have turned down a one-size-fits-all concept in favor of personality, and they have really made the traditions their own. The outfits become a statement about who they are, while the celebration symbolizes the lifestyle that they've chosen together. The restrictions imposed during the Covid-19 pandemic have only strengthened such convictions. Many couples were forced to cancel the celebrations they'd planned, reschedule, and get creative—with incredible results.

The pandemic and lockdowns have also fed into a trend of microweddings. More and more couples are now opting for a ceremony of no more than 50 guests, held in a private setting. Besides their personal, exclusive vibe, small weddings also have certain practical upsides, such as freeing up a bigger budget per head, so you can invest in an especially elaborate menu, your favorite DJ, or a fantastic fireworks display. Many couples go even further and elope so as to experience their nuptials as an intimate moment between the two of them, without any onlookers, a huge party, or outside pressure.

> "There's nothing to stop you from having exactly the wedding that suits you. These days, we can finally marry whomever, however, and wherever we want."

And then there are couples who plan two celebrations: one for their inner circle, and a second, lavish party a few days or months later. At the same time, modern weddings are gravitating towards environmental awareness and sustainability. Couples are choosing venues that don't require guests to travel far, working with local suppliers, sending out invitations on eco-friendly →

→ paper, and serving wedding banquets made with seasonal produce.

In other words, no matter whether you want to say "I do," be it in the park with just the two of you or a wild surprise party for all your friends and family, there's nothing to stop you from having exactly the wedding that suits you. These days, we can finally marry whomever, however, and wherever we want. Even if your family members, time-honored tradition, and Hollywood are whispering in your ear, you don't have to have a textbook wedding for anyone else's sake. Lots of couples are throwing off the shackles of convention, striking out on their own path, and—when they decide to get married—doing it their way.

> "Lovebirds from the farthest corners of the Earth have come up with their very own vision of a dream wedding."

Lots of wedding planners actually specialize in unusual weddings and can arrange fantastic celebrations ranging from outdoor ceremonies to action-based themes. For such professionals, no distance is too far, no mountain too high, and no dream too fantastical. At the same time, it's perfectly possible to arrange a unique wedding all by yourself. Whether you're into music, a certain lifestyle, or sports, a shared passion for something forms a unique and wonderful foundation to build upon. *What a Wedding!* showcases a lot of DIY ideas that are easy to adapt for your own celebration.

Amid all of the excitement, it's important to remember that being able to freely choose your life partner is something that not everyone can enjoy. UNICEF estimates that around 700 million women—and yes, men, too—are in forced marriages. In many parts of the world, marriage doesn't equate to love. This is all the more reason to prize your union, which is entered into freely and with a loving heart, as something very precious indeed. The good news is that more and more countries around the world are now permitting same-sex marriages, allowing people in love to celebrate their feelings for one another openly.

Love knows no bounds, as the many happy couples in *What a Wedding!* can attest. Lovebirds from the farthest corners of the Earth have come up with their very own vision of a dream wedding. Many of the couples featured in this book mixed traditions from two different continents or cultures. Others transformed unusual places into incredible party venues, honored their shared history, or surprised their guests with personal touches. And they continue to be an inspiration long after their big day, as they were true to themselves and made their wedding their very own.

What a Wedding! is intended to get you thinking creatively about your own personal vision for your wedding day. So share another kiss and top up that champagne glass: Here's to the happy couple!

Marianne Julia Strauss is the author and co-editor of What a Wedding! *She is planning her own wedding celebration, which will take place in Yosemite National Park, surrounded by family and close friends. Ultimately, she knows that the best kind of wedding is the one that makes you happy!*

Previous double-page spread Happy nuptials celebrate their big day in Los Angeles; drawing up invitations will be among the first items on your checklist.
This double-page spread Expressive details like abundant colorful flowers and makeup will add drama to your wedding; the couple pictured above chose to have their wedding ceremony in Patagonia.

Make Your Big Day Truly Yours!

A guide to decisions big and small for making your celebration unique

Feeling daunted? That's only natural. But planning your wedding together can be really fun, we promise! The following guide takes you through the things to consider for your big day, answers questions, and points out alternatives to the classic celebration. Essentially, it's all about making your big day truly yours!

Above Whether you are celebrating in the great outdoors or in your own garden, Champagne brings a fair serving of glamour to any venue!
Top left Your vows will be especially deep and meaningful if you have composed them yourself.
Center left Make sure to agree your wedding song with your DJ, and specify what type of musical genres you like and what's a real no-go for you.
Bottom left In case the weather has any rainy surprises in store, make sure you are ready with a Plan B that includes umbrellas and even somewhere you can dodge the showers.

9

Above Unusual ideas such as this floating café will make your wedding unforgettable for you and your guests.
Top right A wedding just for the two of you? Of course. Every moment of your special day is just for you both.
Center right If you book a good photographer, you will be rewarded with dreamy pictures like this one.
Bottom right Even the bridal bouquet is part of the outfit, so match the style of flowers to your bridal gown and colour scheme.

Who, Where, and How?

Do you want to get married with just your nearest and dearest in attendance, surrounded by all your friends, or just the two of you? And where: in your own backyard, at an amusement park, or on your favorite island? Do you want a religious, secular, or registry office wedding? Flip through the different weddings here and see if anything grabs your attention. Which celebrations, settings, and arrangements really speak to both of you? Talk about what you'd like, note down the preferences that you have in common, and come up with some ideas!

"Mood boards help you to visualize your dream ambience. Gather photos of venues, outfits, and styling you like, and think about the details, from decorations to paper napkins."

From All-Inclusive to DIY

There are any number of amazing wedding planners out there who can help you organize your big day, whether as a whole package or by handling certain aspects. They work with a network of caterers, venues, florists, and decorators to ensure that your wedding runs like clockwork. Having a master of ceremonies works well if you're planning a large wedding, as it frees you up to relax and concentrate on just enjoying yourself. Or would you like to organize the whole thing yourselves? In that case, draw up a schedule, take up any offers of help from family and friends, and start with the biggest decisions. You may well find that more ideas and solutions suggest themselves quite naturally from there.

"Under the hashtag #weddingplanner on Instagram, you can find an amazing choice of professional wedding planners and inspirational pictures, from table decorations to photo poses."

Above Search using the term unique weddings for instance, to find inspiration for coordinated—and yet unusual—styling.
Top left Are you hiring a wedding planner? Great! They will make sure that you can focus on the celebration on your big day.
Center left Whether you go for a posy wildflowers or a professionally created bouquet, the flowers you choose will have a huge effect on the ambience.
Bottom left Make your wedding day exceptional! A passion for the unusual will provide variety and unforgettable wedding photos.

Above Elegance attracts elegance: the venue should reflect your style just as much as the outfits and the decor.
Top right If space or your budget only run to a wedding meal for a small number of guests, invite the other people you want around you to party afterwards.
Center right You can find classic wedding venues such as country estates, backyards, or mansions on rental websites, too.
Bottom right And try thinking about more unusual venues, too. Can you imagine your celebration in your favorite gallery or the botanical garden?

The Venue

Speaking of big decisions, the biggest of them all is where you want your celebration to take place. This will come down to the permitted number of guests and the options for catering, entertainment, and decoration. Ballrooms, boats, and other popular venues are often booked out well in advance, so make sure that you plan this aspect first. Once you've confirmed your reservation, you'll have the date for your wedding.

There are also myriad possibilities for holding your celebration outdoors. Remember that you usually need a permit for public places like national parks, and make sure that you have a backup plan in case of bad weather.

"Can't decide? Then plan
for a change of venue.
After a Champagne reception
on the pier, hold the
wedding party in the restaurant
on the dunes, for instance."

Budget

We can't pretend budget planning is particularly romantic, but it's important nonetheless. Weddings run the gamut from a little celebration with just the two of you to a small-scale party with a few family members and friends at your local restaurant, all the way through to a huge party with hundreds of guests. In other words, you could spend anywhere from $100 to $100,000.

It's absolutely possible to do things at a relatively low cost, even if you have a lot of guests: think backyard wedding with homemade salads, your best friend staffing the barbecue, and a kick-ass playlist. If you're opting for a large wedding with all the bells and whistles, you'll have to pay for the wedding planning, the cost of hiring and decorating the venue, catering for the reception and party, the drinks and the wedding cake, the entertainment, invitations and place cards, transportation, and a photographer, at a minimum.

Bear in mind that the official wedding ceremony also comes with a cost attached, on top of your rings, outfits, and accessories. Having wedding insurance means that you're covered if your celebration cannot take place for unexpected reasons. It is also a good idea to set aside 10% of your available budget for unexpected costs.

And one last thing: age-old custom dictates that the bride's parents pay for the wedding, but this is considered very outmoded today. Parents and family members may nevertheless offer some financial support, which is always welcome. If this applies to you, make sure that everyone has a clear idea of exactly who is paying for what, and how much they are contributing.

Above Money not an issue? Congratulations! The good news for everyone else is that it's possible to do a more cost-effective version of many of these wedding looks.
Top left A wedding just for the two of you? Cue: elopement—romantic, but not nearly so heavy on the budget.
Bottom left, left The deep greens of nature or colorful graffiti—decorations that won't cost you a cent.
Bottom left, right Are you dying for this wedding arch on Pinterest? Then indulge your dreams and invest in an unforgettable ambience.

17

Above If you have children or want to include them in the ceremony, let them help choose their outfits, then everyone is happy.
Top right Choose complementary accessories to create a super-coordinated atmosphere to surround and unite you as a couple.
Center right Fashion for the groom comes out of hiding! And it's more varied than ever.
Bottom right Rock 'n' roll will never die! The stage is yours on your wedding day, so grab the limelight.

Fashion

It's never too early to start thinking about what you're going to wear! The good news is that wedding fashion is more diverse than ever these days: individuality and different body types are positively celebrated. Take your cue from your wedding venue and make sure that the styles you choose don't clash, but bear in mind that many wedding gowns take up to 8 months from the first appointment to final delivery. Plan accordingly! Check out the Fashion section on p. 92 for what you should wear for your first dress fitting, plus accessories for the groom.

"Modern wedding fashions
celebrate every type of love and body,
thank goodness. You can mix
age-old fashion rules with your own
personal style and individual
accessories to emphasize the things
you love most."

Be My Guest

Who do you really want at your wedding? And let's be honest: who *don't* you want there? This day is about you. Citing budget constraints and a lack of space are explanations that everyone will accept. Consider whether your wedding is child-friendly—and if it isn't, make sure to give parents enough notice so they can arrange for childcare. If you're having a traditional ceremony, think of who you'd like to be your witnesses, bridesmaids, and groomsmen. If you'd like the children of family and friends to be flower girls or ring bearers, get in touch to ask them.

If you're planning a big party, let the planner or your caterer know the exact number of guests well in advance, and plan in a couple of extra meals—who knows which of your friends will fall madly in love between now and then? Make sure that all of your guests have overnight accommodation booked, and arrange transportation to the ceremony if necessary. Are you doing traditional invitations? Then send out a save-the-date to all of your guests, followed by official wedding invitations, with a request to RSVP promptly. Be sure to ask about dietary restrictions with your invitations to avoid any unpleasant surprises for your guests on the big day.

"Prepare yourself for a couple of gatecrashers as well as for the no-shows. Think of your wedding plan as more of a guide, and you will offload a heap of stress."

Marisa & Janette

INVITE YOU TO THEIR WEDDING
NOVEMBER 30TH, 2019
TULUM, MEXICO

CEREMONY | RECEPTION
MÍA BEACH CLUB | HOTEL TIKI TIKI
4:30 PM | TO FOLLOW

Above Your invitations give your guests the first indication of where the journey will take them.
Top left Make sure your invitations include all the important information, and check it all over, twice!
Center left It looks great if all the wedding stationery is coordinated, with the menus matching the invitations, too.
Bottom left And it doesn't have to be a traditional shape. Creative shapes make a lasting impression and are just plain fun.

Above You want to look good, even at the courthouse. Match your outfits and enchant your family and friends with your coordinated look.
Top right Either leave a couple of days between the courthouse ceremony and the main celebration...
Center right ...or arrange both on the same day and start celebrating as soon as the ink on the official papers is dry!
Bottom right Your ceremony will be uniquely personal if you compose your own vows, so that they say just what it is you love about each other.

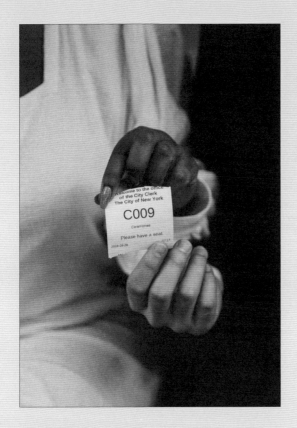

The Ceremony

In your initial conversation with your wedding officiant, discuss what you'd like as part of the ceremony. There tends to be set rites for most religious ceremonies, but this can often be customized a little by personal arrangement. In addition to your vows, would you like to include a reading that means something to you or have an artist perform? These things can all be woven in. The right choice of music really adds to the atmosphere, whether you're in your back garden, a mosque, or a library. See p. 212 for enchanting decoration ideas for large and small ceremonies alike, plus the party afterwards.

"Feeling jittery about saying
'I do'? Everyone does.
It may help to think about the
millions of happy couples
who have overcome this moment
before you."

Entertainment

If you're having a big celebration, book a band or a DJ, or create your own playlist for the ceremony, the reception meal, and the wild party to follow. Would any of your friends be able to provide some entertainment? Put them in charge of the music, or ask particularly eloquent siblings, parents, and friends to give speeches at your reception. Are you both into stand-up comedy or firework displays? Then hire an artist who can make that a part of your day! Setting up a special play area or putting on a show for any children attending will be greatly appreciated by the kids and their parents alike—it could be as simple as hiring a magician or providing lots of toys. Last but not least, having the right entertainment will provide lots of subject matter for great photographs. Look around for a wedding photographer whose work chimes with the style you're looking for, and discuss the shots you'd like in advance.

"If you're having a big celebration, book a band or a DJ, or create your own playlist for the ceremony, the reception meal, and the wild party to follow."

Above The music and entertainment can make or break the party! A good mix of old favorites and a few surprises has stood the test of time.
Top left On your special day, you are there to entertain your guests. Build the suspense, and don't let all the secrets out at once.
Center left Live music is guaranteed to create a good atmosphere, the promise of compelling entertainment, and a full dance floor.
Bottom left Does your four-legged friend steal every heart? Then give him or her the prestigious duty of ring-bearer.

Garden Party with Tents, Hammocks, and a Bar

After their charming country wedding in Brandenburg, Germany, Janine and Jonas danced under starry skies and camped in the garden with all their guests

Above Your wedding cake is an important cast member on your special day. Let your baker advise you in detail, but insist on a full cost breakdown.
Left Details such as these two different chairs or the little tree stump make all the difference. Flower petals make the boho atmosphere just perfect.

Janine and Jonas knew how they wanted their wedding to be: a relaxed country celebration under bright blue skies. And when they visited the enchanting Butterfly Garden near Berlin, they knew that they'd found their venue, too. Together, the couple and the events team transformed the 1.25-acre parkland into a bohemian dreamscape, where the wedding party spent a glorious afternoon following the ceremony. In blazing sunshine, the guests wove pretty flower crowns, challenged each other to games of Viking chess, and relaxed on cushions and picnic blankets around the homemade bar. Everyone indulged in antipasti and quaffed Crémant sparkling wine until the wedding dinner was served in the barn. After applauding heart-warming speeches and dancing through the night, the guests camped out in the garden, waking to the smell of fresh coffee the next morning.

Create a boho atmosphere

Want to celebrate like Janine and Jonas? Conjure up your own boho vibe with lots of colorful lounge areas, cushions, flowers, streamers, and pretty picture frames. A teepee or a self-built bar would make an eye-catching centerpiece.

Above Stacked wood creates a rustic effect and smells amazing, too.
Below Tip for the bartender: always have more ice on hand than you'll need.
Left A love quote helps your guests to tune in to your wavelength.

Above The boutonniere has the same flowers as the bridal bouquet.
Bottom Little cards like these make the meal more personal.
Right Don't want to make too much noise? Then tie balloons to the car instead of tin cans.

How to Find the Right Venue

An indispensable guide to choosing your own dream venue

The possibilities are simply endless when choosing a location for your wedding; a rooftop terrace, ski slope, or a backyard are just a few examples. Remember that your location doesn't have to impress anyone; it's just you who needs to be happy with it. And most of all, your guests want to see you relaxed and content. You can't go wrong with proper preparation, your own checklist, and useful tips from French wedding planner Camille de Luca.

Above You don't have to fly halfway around the world to find dream settings. But you could!
Top left Imagine the venue as the set for your very own movie. What ideas are going through your head?
Center left Pinterest and Instagram are great, but they can stress you out. Don't get caught up looking for perfection.
Bottom left Tip: International blogs like Green Wedding Shoes or La Mariée aux Pieds Nus are stuffed full of great ideas.

Above With a bit of patience, you can find small oases like this one. Focus your big-city search on roof terraces.
Top right Almost any location you have fond memories of could be a possible wedding venue.
Center right Not every venue has an SEO-optimized web presence. So, for your local search, use the map view on Google Maps, too.
Bottom right It may be worth investing more in the venue, as especially beautiful places don't need as much decoration.

Something for Every Budget

Are you looking to plan a wedding without splashing the cash, but want it to be no less special? Gaby and Timah (p. 188) got married on the stoop of a house! But if you're planning a huge celebration complete with a ceremony, reception, and evening party, make sure you secure your venue well in advance. "The best locations are often booked out two years in advance," says Camille, who arranged Vannak and Mathieu's heavenly wedding in a castle hotel on the Mediterranean coast, featured on p. 166.

Wonderful, budget-friendly alternatives include that pretty restaurant around the corner where you had your first date or a colorful café with a garden terrace. In the restaurant trade, events tend to be booked based on a minimum spend per head, rather than an expensive rental fee. At the same time, this gives you a venue that, like a hotel, already has everything in place. You can make the most of a wide selection of dishes and drinks, plus—if you want them—trained service staff. It all helps to make preparing for your celebration that much easier.

"Wonderful budget-friendly options might include that pretty restaurant around the corner—perhaps you had your first date there?"

Quirky Wedding Venues

A botanical garden, factory hall, or beautiful library can all be transformed into magical venues with the help of your wedding planner or close friends. "Public spaces like parks and museums tend to be relatively inexpensive to rent, but they may have to remain open to other visitors at the same time," says Camille. "Besides offering a spectacular backdrop, lots of national parks also issue usage permits at a very reasonable price." Some venues have their own wedding planner on hand to help you with the preparations. Do you want to combine your vows with an unforgettable vacation? Carolin and Bernd's beach wedding on p. 66 shows how you can pull off an amazing destination wedding on a modest budget. Tip: When looking for affordable accommodation for your loved ones, search for boutique hotels or house rentals. Whatever you choose, your guests will welcome some instructions on how to get there, recommendations of places to stay, and information about the destination.

"A secret lake,
a beautifully decorated circus
tent, or a theme park—
there are some special places that
just give you goosebumps."

Above Put your guests at the heart of the ceremony and you will create lasting memories for everyone.
Top left This is a day just for you and your love for each other. Make it a forever memory that will warm your hearts in years to come.
Center left And if this forever memory involves an enchanted Caribbean island, then you really have it made!
Bottom left Does tradition mean a lot to you? Many religious buildings are now more open than ever, and will be happy to go along with your ideas.

41

Above Sometimes more really is more. If your budget can stand it, then just let rip.
Top right An ambience where your style runs right through everything can be really successful. Tinsel? Yes, tinsel!
Bottom right, left Hotels and event venues set the style and will often provide wedding packages that include decor, catering, and service.
Bottom right, right Have a specific restaurant or bar in mind? Then why not spend an evening there in advance
and take an undercover look to see whether the ambience and service are what you are looking for?

Checklist

Do you already have a venue in mind? Brilliant! But whether it's a restaurant in the countryside, an art gallery, or a techno club, be sure to go through your checklist before setting things in motion.

Before you visit the venue, it's a good idea to get the key details via email or on the phone. Would the space work with your wedding concept? Is there enough—or too much—space for your guests? If you're planning a wedding dinner, discuss the cost of food, equipment, and service with the in-house restaurant or caterer.

How easy is it to get to the venue? Is there parking on-site—and is it free?—or are there public transportation connections nearby? Ask how accessible the venue is, and make sure it won't cause any issues for guests with limited mobility. Are there charming places to stay in the immediate vicinity? Check whether there are enough rooms available on the date of your wedding, or organize a shuttle service to alternative accommodation.

"What does the venue allow? Can the DJ unload his equipment at the front door, and can the florist decorate it to get the look you want? Check whether you can light candles, throw confetti, or turn the music up loud," advises Camille. "Will someone from the venue be on-site the whole time? When will the celebrations go on until, and what will it cost to clean up at the end? Will the rental incur additional obligatory costs?" Pin down what's included in the cost of hiring the venue, and get any agreements in writing. If you have any questions, just ask! Online reviews are a good indicator of the venue's dependability and track record of sticking to agreements.

Outdoors

If you're planning a celebration in a private setting or outdoors, then you'll need to think not just about having the items you want in place, but also an electricity supply and enough outlets for lighting, music, and keeping food warm and drinks chilled. Any technical equipment will need to be kept dry. A marquee or awning will protect the buffet and wedding cake from any rain. "If you're planning an open-air wedding, you should also have a good back-up in case of bad weather. That way, you can always opt for plan B without any extra stress on the day," says Camille, who does this even for large outdoor weddings.

    If you're planning an outdoor celebration, check ahead of time that the spot can be set up the way you want. Lay out picnic blankets and a few comfortable chairs, pack mosquito spray, and be sure to leave this little patch of Earth as you found it. Or you could make like Emily and Calvin on p. 194, who settled on a brilliant compromise between indoors and outdoors. Follow your heart, listen to your wedding planner, and most importantly, consult your checklist, to make your venue the perfect setting for your vows, no matter where it is!

"In your outdoor wedding emergency kit, don't forget to include insect repellant, a reliable taxi service, and a Plan B in case of bad weather!"

Above The advantage of a garden wedding is that if it's wet or windy, you can easily transfer indoors.
Top right A ceremony in the great outdoors requires careful preparation, but it will repay your care with unforgettable moments.
Center right Many wedding planners specialize in organizing elopements or destination weddings just for the two of you.
Bottom right Just type the name of the area you want into Google and search for that along with "wedding planner" and "elopement."

A Fall Wedding by Golden Candlelight

Achnagairn Castle in the Scottish
Highlands was the dream venue for Adriana
and Neil's elegant and rustic wedding

Above Florists are true magicians and will fashion stunning bridal bouquets like is from your favorite flowers.
Left The groom traditionally wears a boutonniere to match the bride's bouquet. And of course, he wears it on the left, the same side as his beating heart!

If you choose Bonfire Night as the date of your wedding in the UK, then it's only fitting that you say "I do" by the light of a warm fire. Adriana and Neil got married in front of 80 guests in the ballroom of Achnagairn Castle, Scotland, with countless candles twinkling all around. A fall-themed floral arrangement in warm pastel and red tones stood resplendent behind the couple and served as a backdrop for the traditional ceremony, in place of the usual altar. A local florist used the same blooms to create the lush arch of flowers at the entrance to the hall, as well as Adriana's bridal bouquet, Neil's boutonniere, and the floral crowns worn by the bridesmaids. The entire look was inspired by a mood board of photos, ideas, and favorite colors that Adriana had put together beforehand.

Create a wedding newspaper

Adriana and Neil had the inspired idea of putting together their own wedding newspaper. Besides the check-in and breakfast times, you could print the story of how you got to know each other, the weather forecast, or a crossword puzzle with clues relating to the two of you!

Above Sparklers are always a sure sign that romance is in the air.
Bottom The flowers in the bridal bouquet turn up again and again...
Right ... and also adorn the magnificent flower arrangement above the mantelpiece.

A Wedding in Traditional Austrian Dress

Maria and Alex held their traditional wedding in a
historic courtyard building in Vienna, delighting their guests
with a magical, rustic celebration from a bygone era

Maria & Alex

Above If you want them to, the individual speeches and wedding dance can be some of the most beautiful and intimate moments of your celebration.
Left A wedding in your hometown honors your roots and your family history in a particularly beautiful way.

Maria and Alex's rustic wedding had a dress code with a difference: the 70 guests were asked to wear traditional Austrian dress. In scenes evocative of a bygone era, the wedding party, clad in *dirndls* and *lederhosen,* assembled in the council chamber of Perchtoldsdorf Town Hall to witness the couple say their vows.

Everyone then made their way to the Villa Aurora, where the grounds had been decked out in bucolic style. The quintessentially Austrian celebration continued in the leafy courtyard. Wildflowers stood in pretty glass vases on simple tables, where the stylish guests sat to eat cake.

The evening was rounded off to perfection with a delightfully atmospheric dinner in the old farmyard building, its stone walls, straw-strewn floors, and warm candlelight redolent of the past.

Dresscodes complete the decor

You could adopt a dress code as an extension of your decorative scheme. If you're having a themed wedding, ask your guests to choose their outfits with that in mind. Everyone will get caught up in the special atmosphere that it lends to the whole day.

Above Demonstrate your love with hearts of every hue.
Bottom Put the drinks on ice to keep them chilled and create great decoration, too.
Right A buffet can create a relaxing atmosphere and encourage your guests to talk with one another.

Above If you are folding the napkins yourself, practice it a few times.
Bottom A rustic feel, all from a handful of hay—so simple.
Left A good mix of different table heights adds vibrancy.

A Boho Elopement
in the Caribbean

Laura and Josh wanted to start their honeymoon right after
their wedding, so they opted to get married on the paradise island
of Saint Lucia, with its wild mountains and beaches

Above Is there a cooler way to roll into your new life together than on a skateboard under Caribbean palms?
Left The walk to the wedding site is also symbolic, as you are treading a shared path.

Laura wanted to get married in the mountains; Josh longed for the sea. The little island of Saint Lucia in the Caribbean offered both, and checked another of the couple's boxes: it meant that they could embark on their honeymoon the moment they were married, without having to go elsewhere. Saint Lucia turned out to be the perfect choice: with its precipitous peaks, rainforests, waterfalls, fishing villages, volcanic beaches, and hidden diving spots, the island is a veritable miniature paradise. On the big day itself, the couple walked up into the mountains, Laura dressed in her wedding gown and boots and Josh looking good in a

floral tie and sneakers. They exchanged rings against the spectacular backdrop of the Pitons before skating down jungle roads to the sea, strolling through the surf, and beginning their honeymoon then and there.

Combine your ideas

Laura and Josh show how you can pool ideas together to come up with a wedding that works for both of you. The answer might be a bit unconventional—nothing is off the table! And if you're lucky, you might find a compromise as lovely as a little island in the Caribbean.

Above The sounds of the sea always intensify emotions.
Bottom Whatever you do, don't forget to keep a copy of your vows!
Right They will always sweeten your memories.

A Small Beach Wedding in the Algarve

Carolin and Bernd had an open-air ceremony on the seashore in Aljezur, Portugal, in front of an improvised wedding arch fashioned from two sandy surfboards

Above A simple ceremony with guests sitting on beach towels shows that an enchanting wedding is possible on any budget.
Left Bernd and Carolin shared their love of surfing with their family at this quiet beach wedding in Portugal.

Carolin and Bernd wanted a small-scale wedding with everything that they loved: traveling, family, a wild coastline, picturesque beaches, amazing food, and incredible views. Portugal was just what they were looking for. The German couple invited their family and closest friends on a trip to the western Algarve coast. The beach at Monte Clérigo provided the ideal spot for the ceremony, with a couple of rocky crags creating an intimate atmosphere and sheltering the party from the wind and sun. Before the magic moment, the guests laid out a huge heart made of handpicked flowers and pebbles in the sand. Instead of a wedding arch, Carolin and Bernd borrowed two surfboards from the little beachside restaurant where the laid-back reception dinner took place afterwards.

Free in the great outdoors

Small outdoor weddings don't usually require official registration. Make like Carolin and Bernd and decorate the spot only with what you find there, leaving it as beautiful as you found it!

Above and bottom The couple invited their closest friends and family
to this quiet destination wedding among the sand and the surf—no shoes required!

Katja & Tom

A Beautiful Wedding on a Lake at Sunrise

The entire wedding party paddled
out to a floating platform on the Latvian
lake of Kala Ezers

Above Flowers and stems should always be completely dry so they don't leave any stains on your dream dress.
Left Saying "I do" at sunrise, the start of a new day, carries an especially beautiful significance.

Why get married by a lake when you could get married on the lake itself? Katja and Tom invited their guests to spend a "ferns and waves"-themed weekend together in the Latvian countryside. They rented a couple of charming wooden huts beside the lake of Kala Ezers, and everyone pitched in with the decorations.

Katja and Tom wanted their wedding to be like a miniature festival, Wes Anderson style. They embellished their vision with all sorts of amazing little details, even making the train journey from Riga, 160 miles away, into a kind of scavenger hunt for their family and friends to set the tone for the weekend. At the little branch line station, a retro Soviet bus stood ready to chauffeur the arriving guests to the wedding venue. Everyone retired to their huts for an early night—after all, they had to be up before sunrise the next morning! While it was still pitch dark, the party set out across the waters of Kala Ezers in their kayaks, paddling past a floating café to reach the simple platform that would host the wedding ceremony. The bridal couple followed a little later in a beautifully adorned wedding boat.

Musicians played softly in the background. Katja and Tom said their vows just as the sun peeked over the horizon. In the dawn light, the crowd headed back to the lakeshore for a champagne breakfast and then back to bed, before rising again at midday to carry on partying, eating, dancing—well-rested and still basking in the glow of their enchanting experience that morning.

Relaxed introductions

Will your event mark the first time that your family and friends meet each other? Then take a page from Katja and Tom's book! On arrival at the train station, their guests, who came from all over the world, were picked up in a charming old Soviet bus, ensuring an instant party atmosphere on board.

Above Life jackets? Yes, of course, safety first.
Bottom Music is the voice of your celebration.
Left Stay right next to one another and you will get the most out of every moment.

Top left There are thousands of enchanting ways
to draw attention to the seating plan.
Top right Repetition helps to create a harmonious impression.
These blueberries have been used as decoration on the cake
and again (*below*) in small bowls as a snack.
Above The ferns have been placed in matching planters.
Right The candles here match the flower
arrangements and the bridal bouquet.
Opposite Your meal could include one or two special
effects such as soup over a real fire, but of course
you always need to keep safety in mind.

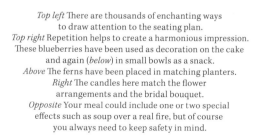

79

Above If your eloquent friends offer to make speeches, that's perfect.
Bottom Make sure that any snacks or finger food aren't sticky.
Left Invest in a great photographer and you will be rewarded with priceless pictures.

Sailing Away to Say "I do"

After a photoshoot in the most beautiful corners
of Barcelona, Richard and Daniel sailed out to sea and said
their vows on the waves, against a golden sunset

Above Getting married at sea doesn't mean you have to do without traditional elements such as the wedding cake.
Left Meet the person giving your wedding address online or in person before the day to make sure the chemistry works between you.

Richard and Daniel could imagine no finer spot for their wedding than Barcelona, with its striking architecture and large LGBTQ+ community. The Florida couple used a local wedding planner, who organized a sailboat for the ceremony and booked a Spanish team of photographers whose style they particularly liked.

On the big day, they wandered through the Gothic Quarter and the Parc de la Ciutadella with their photographer, discovering dreamy settings like historic alleyways and romantic little gardens. As the sun began to set in the late afternoon, they headed to the harbor,

where the chartered sailboat and wedding officiant were waiting. After saying their vows, Richard and Daniel celebrated with Champagne and cake before sailing off together into the sunset.

Make time for photographs

If you want to capture your favorite settings in their very best light and ensure that your wedding pictures turn out well, you need to be mindful of the time of day. The sun is low in the sky in the morning and evening, casting warm tones. And clouds act as a diffuser!

A Dream Wedding in '50 Shades of Green'

At their elegant, bucolic wedding, Upile and Sakhe were
married by the bride's sister, surrounded by color-coordinated
bridesmaids and groomspeople

Above It applies to the bridal bouquet, too: different shades with the same intensity of color almost always make for a harmonious picture.
Left Discuss a few poses for the wedding photos in advance, but go with your impulses, too. The candid shots are often the most genuine.

Upile and Sakhe love plants, so they knew right away that they wanted their Pretoria wedding to feature lots of lush greenery. The outfits worn by the bridesmaids and groomspeople were also picked to chime with the natural look of the celebration. As all of the bridesmaids live in different countries, Upile suggested an olive-colored satin dress from an online retailer and each bridesmaid ordered it in her size. Sakhe's groomsmen—and groomswoman!—matched in bespoke forest-green suits. Amid the abundant eucalyptus, pampas grass, and baby's breath, Upile's sister conducted the ceremony and joined Sakhe and Upile in matrimony, with a heartfelt wish that their love grow, flourish, and blossom, just like the greenery around them.

Sleep on it!

Upile designed her own dream dress, in a soft pink, with the help of a friend. Before that, she had bought a dress on a whim, only to regret it later. Her advice: sleep on a potential purchase for at least one night before making a final decision.

Above Your own signature cocktails will add a touch of glamour.
Bottom Wedding favors are a sweet reminder for guests to take home with them.
Right Tip: Make your way to the altar or bridal arch more slowly than your instinct tells you!

How to Decide on the Outfit

Modern wedding fashion embraces all types of love and body shapes

You've said yes to the big question and are walking around on cloud nine. But it's not long before another big question starts running through your head, and this time the answer isn't nearly as obvious: *What will I wear?* Fortunately, wedding fashion these days is more diverse than ever. Designers are increasingly moving with the times and creating fashion to suit all types of love and body shapes. Read on for our guide to finding an outfit that expresses you at your radiant best.

Above The dreamy, oversized silhouette combines elegance, reserve, and individuality.
Top left Think about practicality when you are choosing your outfit, and have a matching sweater or cape on hand for those cooler evenings.
Center left A classic suit makes a great canvas for individual accessories, such as statement socks or a tie in your favorite color.
Bottom left Are hats your thing? There's no reason why you shouldn't wear one for your wedding.

Above Films such as the classic *Thelma and Louise* are a great source of ideas for your outfits.
Top right Have the florist of your choice mock up a couple of examples of floral accessories such as flower wreaths for you.
Center right Do you have a specific period, such as the '70s, in mind? Then make sure you carry the theme throughout the event.
Bottom right Matching suits take the partner look to a whole new level and make it absolutely clear that you two belong together.

#inspiration

"The best way of pinpointing the right look is to create a mood board," advises Franziska Burgert. The Berlin-based designer has been designing custom bridal fashion since 2015 and is well aware of the questions that newly engaged couples are likely to be asking. "You can find a huge selection on Instagram and Pinterest by entering keywords like #weddingdress, #groomstyle, #queerwedding, or #curvybride. But make sure that you're mainly pinning looks that suit the style and venue for your wedding!" Tip: Most places get cooler in the evening, so give some thought to a cape, a stole, or even a hoodie!

"Wedding blogs on sites like Pinterest and Instagram are a great source of ideas alongside your own closet. Pin all the wedding dresses, suits, shoes, and accessories that catch your eye so you can start to recognize key themes."

Her Style

You might be hankering after a '70s vibe, dreaming of a princess dress, or toying with something altogether different. "Diaphanous elements and narrowly cut wedding dresses with plunging necklines are very popular at the moment," says Franziska. "Self-confident brides no longer have to compromise on style; they can wear whatever they like." Some women opt for a suit or an oversized dress, which go for the cool factor over overt sexiness. The classic A-line remains a perennial favorite, as it flatters every type of figure, from XS to XL. Choose the shade of white that complements your skin tone, or go for a completely unconventional color! As you can see from the brides in this book, there's no right or wrong way to make your way down the aisle, as long as you can walk, move and dance comfortably and confidently.

"Self-confident brides don't have to compromise. They can wear whatever they like. Close-fitting wedding clothes that make a striking impression are popular at the moment."

Above As a bride, you can certainly ask your bridesmaids to choose specific colors for their dresses.
Top left Some veils create a magical sensation, made even more beautiful when they shimmer in the brightest colors.
Center left Whether you go for a dress or a suit, your outfit must fit perfectly. Choose a one-off or have alterations made by your favorite tailor.
Bottom left The classic A-line can be made up in hundreds of styles and fabrics and is sure to have that breathtaking wow factor.

Above Color-coordinating with your groomsmen? Great idea. As the groom, you can stand out
from the crowd by the way you accessorize, as seen here, with a jacket.
Top right You know what suits you. If your wedding outfit is a celebratory variation on your everyday style, then you can be sure that you will look great.
Center right A personal motto embroidered on your sleeve is a great way to individualize your outfit.
Bottom right Vintage can be super stylish. And wearing vintage gives you a really distinctive look.

His Style

Dandy or casual? These days, men have an ever-growing range of looks to choose from. Are you perfectly comfortable in a suit, or more of a relaxed type? What about color: is it charcoal all the way, or do you want to include some colorful accents in your outfit? Whatever you're thinking, discuss it with your bride or groom to ensure that your outfits will work together and look appropriate for the style of your wedding. A formal suit and bow tie are the correct attire for a traditional celebration, but bohemian weddings could feature sturdy boots and a patterned shirt. If you're also looking to make the most of your body type, stick to time-honored fashion diktats, such as wearing a slender tie to elongate your torso, or adding a pocket square for an eye-catching element at chest level.

"The choice of colors, cuts and accessories, shoes, and vintage finds means that today's grooms have as many options as their brides to personalize their wedding outfits."

Salons

If you're buying your outfit from a bridal salon or tailor, arrange your first fitting with plenty of time to spare. If you intend to wear shapewear under your dress, bring a pair to your first fitting. Most salons have order deadlines of six to eight months for dresses and three months for suits. This gives enough leeway for any alterations that you might desire or require. Factor in enough time for adding any extra beads, embroidery, or straps to the dress.

"Buying your wedding dress should be an unforgettably wonderful experience. Take your time to look at lots of bridal salons, sleep on your decision for several nights and only buy from a store where you feel well-attended."

Above Wedding dresses are the romantic playthings of the best designers in the world. If you can afford it, absolute paradise is waiting you.
Top left In the bridal salon, describe where and how you are getting married. Together, you will find just the dress to suit you and your wedding style.
Center left Many bridal salons also carry a range of veils, shoes, garters, and other accessories.
Bottom left What do you like best about your body? Direct the admiring gazes towards your amazing legs or attractive curves.

101

Above We all know that makeup is part of the outfit, and so much the better if his boutonniere picks up the color of your eyeshadow.
Top right Sneakers are in for weddings and are the contemporary update for any suit.
Bottom right, left Sore feet after too much dancing? Dance barefoot, or better yet, change into that spare pair of flats you brought along with you.
Bottom right, right You can have your jacket "engraved" in just the same way as your wedding rings. Your tailor will be pleased to sort out that embroidery for you.

As Individual as You are

Do you want to have your very own outfit custom made? Then research bridal fashion designers and tailors in your local area and arrange an initial consultation. "I always ask every new bride, 'What do you really like about your body?' And then we create the dress around that," says Franziska. "Curvy brides often opt for a beautiful decolleté, for instance, while taller brides might like to showcase their long legs. There really is a dream dress out there for every body type, and they can all be made to match the style of the wedding." The initial consultation usually takes about two hours and is free of charge. If you end up buying, any subsequent consultations are usually costed into the price of the dress.

Tip: It's best to wear nude-colored underwear when trying on your wedding dress, so it won't show through beneath gowns with transparent panels. Bridal studios always have high-heeled shoes that you can wear for the fitting. Avoid wearing makeup, as it can come off on sample gowns.

The groom should also discuss the type of wedding and his preferred suit style with his tailor. Which design will prove most flattering? Waistcoat or traditional tails? Necktie or bowtie? Or keep it casual with neither? Together, you can look at different cuts, fits, and materials to find the suit that will show you off to best effect.

"You can look at different
cuts, fits, and materials
to find the suit that will show
you off to best effect."

Accessories

There are all manner of traditional accessories, but these days you can really go for something a bit different. You might pair a hat with your boho wedding gown, for instance. Bridal accessories like hair decorations, bracelets, or henna patterns tend to complement and emphasize the style of the dress. Similarly, personalized cufflinks, a printed pocket square, or leather suspenders can lend a whole new vibe to a plain suit. Most grooms still like to wear a boutonniere made from the same flowers as the bridal bouquet to symbolize the couple's bond.

Bear in mind the location of your wedding when choosing accessories. A long veil looks amazing as long as there's no wind from behind. That said, ultimately the best accessory of all is the smile on your face!

"The accessories are what makes any outfit. For instance, a shimmering tiara will give your dress a completely different look than wildflowers in your hair."

Above Getting on board the soul train? Bright red heels provide a neat shot of cool for the dreamy outfit.
Top left A patterned tie enlivens the outfit. But make sure you get a style-savvy friend to approve the pattern beforehand.
Center left You will make a fantastically feminine statement by wearing a sensational tiara like this.
Bottom left When you choose your bridal bouquet, think about the colors of your other accessories so that all the colors harmonize.

105

A '70s-Inspired Wedding with a Whole Lot of Soul

Roxanne and Cameron were born to dance,
so they flew in their favorite DJ and a suitcase full of Motown
records for a funk-filled New York party

Above The bride wore bright platform heels, in keeping with the day's 70s theme.
Left Roxanne and Cameron were married at a tiny ceremony at City Hall in Manhattan before heading off to celebrate.

Roxanne and Cameron certainly know how to party. After a civil wedding at Manhattan City Clerk's Office Marriage Bureau and a rooftop ceremony at the Bathhouse Studios, the pair threw a full-on dance party, with plenty of soul, funk, and R&B. For inspiration, Roxanne took the advice of her wedding planner and filled her Pinterest board not with pictures of other weddings, but with all sorts of things that chimed with the couple's style. The whole celebration radiated the warm yet hip vibe of '70s New York. The highlight of the reception had to be the Motown hits played by Roxanne and Cameron's favorite DJ, Reverend P, who flew in specially from Paris. What better way to mark the occasion than dancing to Marvin Gaye's "How Sweet It Is (To Be Loved By You)"?

Base your theme on shared passions

Do you want your big day to be the perfect reflection of your style, like Roxanne and Cameron? The couple filled their mood board with everything that appealed to them, from printed shopping bags to a picture of a retro airport terminal!

Above left The towering cake before being enjoyed by guests.
Above right Roxanne's hairstylist placed baby's breath in her hair to create a gorgeous floral crown.
Bottom and right For their reception, the couple took inspiration from Solange,
the old TWA terminal at JFK, bodega flower stands, Motown parties in Paris, and more.

A Punchy Wedding Full of Handmade Touches

This Los Angeles couple loves rainbows, color and making art—at their wedding, all three come together in an explosion of bright hues and DIY delight.

Above The bride's bouquet neatly fit the colorful theme with big pink blooms and squiggly stems.
Left The venue was selected for its sustainability credentials, as well as the many plants that it houses.

From the tie-dyed napkins to the rainbow quilt to even the bride's hair—every surface at this wedding was imbued in color and vibrance. Gina and Alex tied the knot at Smog Shoppe in Culver City, California, a plant-filled space that runs on solar power. The wedding was filled with handmade touches, crafted by the bride, who runs a knitwear brand, and groom, who works as a freelance film handler and artist. The couple's love of color was everywhere for the guests to enjoy. No less enjoyable were the breads and baked goods served at the reception, which were made by Gina's father who owns a local bakery and restaurant.

The detail makes the moment

Each napkin was tie-dyed by the couple, and the scraps were used to create an eye-catching quilt and photo backdrop. If you're going with DIY, save your scraps! Like with Gina and Alex, they can be reused to create something beautiful.

Gina & Alex

Above left The handmade quilt was a punchy backdrop to the place settings.
Above right The wedding favors were a pair of socks emblazoned with the words "everything and lots of it," which is how the groom orders his sandwiches.

Blending Cultures and Traditions

Solbee and Glenn wove Korean and Australian traditions together
for their wedding in Mokpo, South Korea, which celebrated both their love
for one another and their respective cultural backgrounds

Above Does your partnership cross cultures? Use this wonderful opportunity to celebrate all the different aspects of your life at your wedding.
Left This way you'll both be ambassadors for your respective cultural heritages, and you'll show everyone just what makes your country so special.

From the outset, Solbee and Glenn knew that they wanted their wedding to be a celebration of their different backgrounds. The couple, who live in Australia, decided to have a traditional celebration in Solbee's homeland of South Korea, but with western details deftly woven into the ceremony. In accordance with the age-old Korean custom, Glenn presented his new mother-in-law with the *jeon-an-rye,* symbolic wooden geese. Not to be outdone, Solbee's father-in-law had prepared a speech in impeccable Korean. After the marriage ceremony in traditional *hanbok* attire, Solbee and Glenn changed into Western outfits. Solbee paired her wedding dress, which she had designed herself, with her Australian mother-in-law's earrings—her "something borrowed." The gemstones matched the glorious blue skies on the day, auguring boundless joy amid time-honored tradition.

Entwine your different cultures

Solbee and Glenn show how you can intertwine elements from different cultures to create a beautiful celebration. Think about the customs and rituals that are important to you, and design a wedding that represents both of you in equal measure.

Above Respect for tradition also means you are respecting your own family history.
Bottom A ceremony that honors these traditions will make you happy...
Right ... and the rest of your family, too.

A Danish Wedding with a Lighthouse Standing Witness

Countryside, art, and city all in one day! After an elegant ceremony
on the coast of Copenhagen, Sibylle and Ryan spent the
afternoon with their guests at the Louisiana Modern Art Museum

Above The moment when you see each other for the first time in your wedding dress and wedding suit is something truly romantic.
Left Whether it's natural, elegant, or modern, the backdrop to your wedding is significant in setting the scene for your celebration.

Why choose between nature, art, and urban chic when you can have all three? Sibylle and Ryan invited their closest friends and family first to Denmark's Baltic Sea coast, where they said their vows under the benevolent eye of a lighthouse. A specially chartered bus then whisked the entire wedding party away to the Louisiana Museum of Modern Art and its gorgeous sculpture park.

When they'd had their fill of everything from Pop Art masterpieces to Nouveau Réalisme, Sibylle, Ryan, and their guests moved on to their final stop of the day in downtown Copenhagen. Here, they were treated to an exquisite wedding meal in a stylish location, followed by an unforgettable party that went on well into the night.

Plan ahead for a venue change

Sibylle and Ryan demonstrate how you can make your wedding celebration a series of exciting highlights: choose locations with a high entertainment factor and weave your personal interests into the plan for the day!

Above Inspire your guests with highlights such as a visit to a lighthouse.
Bottom Arrangements of white flowers create an elegant and subtle effect.
Right This striking wedding dress complements the setting perfectly.

Above Finger food is always much appreciated at any wedding.
Bottom Ensure that the flower arrangements and bridal bouquet complement one another.
Left The wedding table obviously picks up the color concept beautifully.

Laurence & Ayoub

An Enchanting Celebration Under Morocco's Starry Skies

Laurence and Ayoub combined time-honored
wedding traditions with their own ideas
to create an incredible two-night celebration
under Morocco's starry skies

Above Ask your maid of honor to bring along a small emergency kit with tissues, lip gloss, safety pins, etc., just in case.
Left Special bar carts like this look super decorative, as well as providing refreshments.

Laurence had just moved from Belgium to Morocco with her LRNCE Design Studio when Ayoub made a fleeting visit to Marrakech, his hometown, from Paris. It was inevitable that their wedding three years later would have style, culture, and creativity in abundance.

The couple chose the gorgeous garden of Ayoub's parents' house as the venue for their traditional Moroccan ceremony on the first evening. Laurence repurposed and painted an old horse-drawn carriage to create a watermelon bar. The tables were adorned with candles and ceramics from the bride's own label. During the ceremony, Laurence and Ayoub sat on a pale blue bench, another of the bride's designs, to share a glass of milk and a date with their mothers, as a sign of welcoming each other into their families. The bridal pair made quite an entrance. Ayoub came in riding on a white camel, surrounded by all his friends. Not to be outdone, Laurence arrived in an *ammariya*—an opulently decorated sedan chair carried by four men—to the hip-hop beats of British-Sri Lankan artist M. I. A. The couple and their guests danced into the wee hours of the morning, long after the DJ had taken over from the live band.

The secular ceremony was a more intimate event held on the second evening. Laurence and Ayoub were married at sunset on the roof terrace of the stylish Hotel Tigmi, with their closest friends in attendance. The guests passed around a small ceramic bowl containing the couple's rings and took it in turns to say their wishes for the couple's future happiness. Everyone then celebrated together under the stars, which shone like the French engraving in Laurence's ring—"Sun of my heart."

Your way is the only way

Laurence and Ayoub gave a master class in weaving personal details into their wedding as magical finishing touches. Have your loved ones bless your rings with heartfelt wishes, play hip-hop instead of the standard entrance music, and dare to put your personal stamp on time-honored traditions!

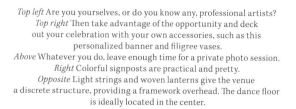

Top left Are you yourselves, or do you know any, professional artists?
Top right Then take advantage of the opportunity and deck
out your celebration with your own accessories, such as this
personalized banner and filigree vases.
Above Whatever you do, leave enough time for a private photo session.
Right Colorful signposts are practical and pretty.
Opposite Light strings and woven lanterns give the venue
a discrete structure, providing a framework overhead. The dance floor
is ideally located in the center.

Above A precise timeline gives you confidence and leaves you free to enjoy the celebration—and the confetti shower.
Left Repetition creates cohesion. The shapes and colors of the wedding table are repeated here.

Above Natural decoration such as the branches in the candle holders and the pretty decoration on the plates are simple and effective.
Right Boom, well it's your day! Lighten up on the tradition with a bit of hip-hop, for instance, like Laurence did.

Open-Air Ceremony in the Wild Forest of the Highlands

Jodi and Zach spent a fabulous week with their closest
friends and family in the Cairngorms National Park, Scotland,
and said "I do" in the middle of the forest

Above Genuine feelings turn your ceremony into an experience—for your guests, as well—and one that will bind you together for good.
Left During the celebrations, always make time just for the two of you to take in everything that has just happened.

As photographer couple The Camerados, Zach and Jodi travel to the most beautiful places in the world. The bewitching Cairngorms National Park amid the Scottish Highlands has always held a special place in their hearts. For their own wedding, they invited their closest friends and family members to go there for a whole week of great food, walking, and revelry in the great outdoors.

The wedding itself was held on a mild spring morning. After breakfasting together at a table decked with fresh wildflowers, the small wedding party made its way into the forest. The gentle rustling of the leaves was the only soundtrack to the ceremony, which was conducted by a dear friend of the couple. Zach and Jodi said their touching vows and then treated their guests to an impromptu ukulele performance.

Celebrating far away

If you like the idea of getting married abroad like Jodi and Zach, then it's a nice gesture to help your guests plan their trips. You could email them packing lists, look up flights and accommodation, and factor in plenty of time for them to get there and settle in.

Above Do you have a shared talent? Make a small display of it.
Bottom The great outdoors gives your celebration an especially personal touch.
Right DIY decorations are often just as good as hiring professionals.

How to Host a Sustainable Wedding

Have you considered the environmental footprint of your wedding?

By now, we're all aware of the pressing need to consider our footprint on the planet. With hundreds of guests flying in, weddings aren't always as sustainable as they can be, and there's always room to improve. You don't need to drill down to the very last detail; a few tweaks can reduce the environmental footprint of your celebration and get your new life together off to a planet-friendly start.

Above Looking for sustainable decorations for your celebration? Make sure to ask your florist for Fairtrade flowers.
Top left Branches you have gathered from your own garden really don't have any ecological footprint.
Center left Did you know that candles are made mainly from paraffin, a by-product of the oil industry?
Even supposedly organic candles made of palm oil, or stearin, are problematic.
Bottom left Biomass, beeswax, soy wax, or canola candles are better, and are about the same low price.

151

Above Discuss with your chosen baker what sort of organic cake you have in mind.
Top right Your own crockery, locally sourced finger food, and glass or paper straws are easy swaps to make things more sustainable.
Center right Use local, independent florists, printers, and graphic designers wherever possible to show that you support local business.
Bottom right Homemade decorations can also be more eco-friendly because they don't require transportation.

Support Your Locals!

Did you know that the average wedding results in around 650 pounds of waste, 60 tons of CO_2, and over 1,200 food miles? "Opting for an eco-accredited wedding venue that won't require most of your guests to travel too far is the most impactful decision you can make," says Jacqueline Deininger, who has planned countless sustainable weddings with her agency, Ja von Herzen.

"Having a local wedding with 100 guests is always going to be more sustainable than a party for 10 guests who have to fly halfway around the world to attend." When it comes to the catering, be mindful of regional produce and put together a seasonal wedding menu. For instance, vegetarian or vegan options tend to be less harmful. Source your meat from a local organic butcher, though, and you'll check both boxes. You could organize in advance for anything left over from the wedding meal to be donated to your nearest municipal food project. Are there any wineries or microbreweries nearby? Wonderful: that's your drinks taken care of! You could also see whether your wedding cake could be made using local, organic, and perhaps even vegan, ingredients.

"Focus on finding
eco-certified venues in the local
area, and try to hire local businesses
to cater and decorate."

Eco Decorations

What do a botanical garden, a forest clearing, and a beach have in common? That's right: they're so exquisite that they need very little decoration to serve as a gorgeous location for your vows. But what if you're getting married in a grand function room or on a rooftop? Then you can still create a natural, eco-friendly vibe with stone, wood, or floral decorations. "By the way, that doesn't mean that you need to plump for a 'vintage' or 'rustic' theme," says Jacqueline. "Savvy pairings of materials can create quite the modern look, even with natural elements." You can have fun hunting down pretty one-off pieces in flea markets and the classifieds, and save yourself a bit of money at the same time. Alternatively, invite everyone over to a crafting session a couple of weeks before the big day. Adorn the tables with local potted plants, pretty little succulents, or easy-care air plants: you can do without elaborate flower arrangements and end up with less waste at the end of the evening. Tip: Use the flowerpots as place cards, too!

For the sake of seabirds and turtles, try to do without balloons. Despite our best intentions, they often end up in the sea. Alternatives to blowing bubbles include dried flowers or biodegradable confetti, which not only looks magical, but also disintegrates into nothing, without leaving any residue.

"Pretty decorations can be 100% eco-friendly. You can really make your wedding greener by using natural petal confetti, vintage decorations, and potted plants instead of cut flowers."

Above In the weeks before your wedding, pick a couple of decorative wildflowers each time you
go out for a walk, dry them upside down, and then use them to decorate your venue.
Top left Organize an event at home with friends, cakes, and cocktails, and craft your decorations together.
Center left Vintage finds from your grandparents' attic or from the flea market can be super decorative.
Bottom left If you are making your decorations yourself, look out for eco-certified materials or use recycled trimmings.

155

Above Rain? It's good for nature, and for your outfits. There are thousands of outfits you could choose, from dresses made of vegan silk to a stylish vintage suit.
Top right Instead of a veil with a high polyester content, why not wear a flower garland made of locally grown flowers?
Bottom right, left Vintage outfits are extra sustainable. Get your tailor service to give your dress or suit that finishing touch.
Bottom right, right The bridal bouquet and the boutonniere can be created from sustainably grown flowers, too.

156

Sustainable from Head to Toe

Your choice of wedding dress and suit can really set the tone for your green wedding, while looking utterly ravishing. With a couple of alterations, a vintage piece can be transformed into your very own dream gown or suit. "If you're set on buying a new dress, then support a local designer if you can, and consider having it made from materials like vegan silk, which is made from pima cotton, agave fibers, or bamboo, rather than the traditional caterpillar cocoons," advises Jacqueline. Think about how you might be able to go on using your dress after the big day, opt for bridal separates, or have your dress dyed once it's all over. Another practical option is to rent your wedding dress or suit for the day. Pair them with Fairtrade accessories and non-leather shoes, and you have yourself a sustainable wedding outfit!

Consider having your wedding rings forged from Fairtrade or recycled gold. Alternatively, if you have old jewelry or family heirlooms that you no longer wear, you could have these melted down and made into your rings. Not only is this the ultimate in sustainability, but it will also make these pieces all the more meaningful. Are you longing for a diamond-studded ring? Then opt for stones accredited as conflict-free, from partners of the Kimberley Process Certification Scheme.

"Have your wedding bands forged out of Fairtrade or recycled gold, and make sure diamonds have conflict-free origin certification."

Stationery

Your invitations are the perfect opportunity to get your guests in the mood for a green wedding. Choose a stylish, environmentally friendly type of paper without foil or gloss elements, and make it clear that you'll be placing a particular emphasis on sustainability at the event. If you're planning to set up a website for your wedding, host it with an eco-friendly provider. Like the invitation, you can print the menu and place cards on paper from sustainable forestry sources.

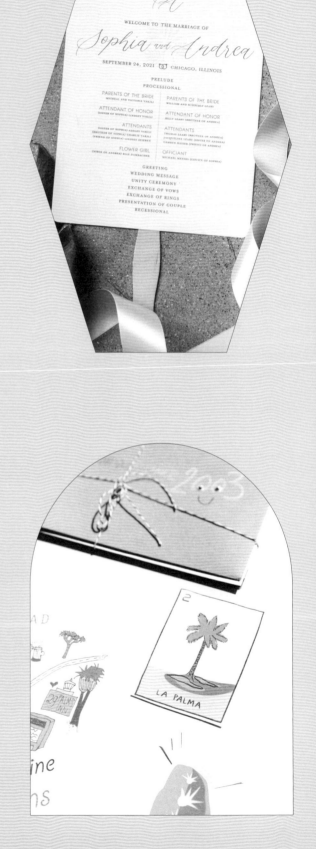

"There is an enormous choice of really beautiful recycled paper and foil-free designs for invitations, menus, and place cards nowadays."

Above Sustainability can be really stylish. This die-cut invitation opens up like a delicate flower.
Top left Did you know that you can get carbon-neutral printing now? You can find out more on the internet by searching for "green printing."
Center left Your choice of crest next to the wording on the invitation is a great way to get your guests tuned into your green wedding.
Bottom left Homemade can be the most environmentally friendly option for stationery, too, if you use sustainable materials.

Rings and Rucksacks: an Elopement in Patagonia

Adri and Eric made their way up into the mountains
first thing in the morning to say "I do" against the stunning
backdrop of the Laguna de los Tres at sunrise

Above A magical mountain panorama like this one requires an equally magical wedding dress from Rue de Seine—and some sturdy walking shoes!
Left If the first few yards of your shared journey look like this, you are sure to have gotten everything just right.

When Adri and Eric came across a few pictures of Patagonia shortly after their engagement, the couple knew right then and there that *this* was where they wanted to get married. At five o'clock on the morning of their wedding, the pair began their hike to the turquoise Laguna de los Tres, with the wedding dress, bridal bouquet, and rings stashed in their rucksacks. Shortly before they arrived, the peaks of the mountains began to glisten and gleam in the light of the rising sun, bathing Adria and Eric in their glow as they reached the edge of the mountain lake. After a warming swig of instant coffee from the Thermos, Adri slipped into her enchanting bridal gown from Rue de Seine, while Eric got the Champagne ready. Against the breathtaking backdrop of the Argentine Andes, the couple said their vows, with the summit of Monte Fitz Roy standing witness.

Follow your own path

Hiking doesn't have to nix a stylish outdoor wedding! Along with their trusty Thermos, Adri and Eric just packed the Champagne, the rings, and the bride's stunning wedding dress in their backpacks.

A Gorgeous Wedding between Cambodia and Canada

Mathieu and Vannak were delighted when
a wedding date unexpectedly opened up
at the Château de Cassis in the south of France,
midway between Cambodia and Canada

Above Following Cambodian tradition, the newlyweds lay their hands on a large cushion, where the traditional bracelets are placed.
Left After the ceremony, their parents are the first to bless them and wish them well. Then all the other married guests congratulate them.

Some years before their actual wedding, Mathieu and Vannak had already begun to come up with enchanting ideas for their celebration. When they visited the historic Château de Cassis on the French Mediterranean coast and learned that a date had suddenly become free, the couple went for it. Together with their French wedding planner, Mathieu and Vannak decided upon a decorative scheme featuring lots of natural greenery and pale shades that would complement the beige-colored stone of the château. The 120 invited guests were asked to dress in pastels. The wedding invitations were adorned with a tropical leaf, which stood for Vannak and his home country of Cambodia, and an apple tree leaf, representing Mathieu and his Canadian homeland.

Mathieu and Vannak blended their own style with traditional elements when it came to their wedding ceremony, too. The couple lifted their favorite hour-long section from the Khmer ritual, which usually spans several days. They also donned traditional Cambodian wedding attire, and paired it with flower garlands. For the secular ceremony, Mathieu and Vannak wore pale suits. The entire wedding party made their way from the foyer of the château hotel onto the spectacular terrace, where the couple exchanged vows against a dreamlike Mediterranean backdrop.

Mathieu and Vannak wanted to be able to focus solely on their love for one another and on their guests, who had come from far and wide, so the couple discussed every last detail with their wedding planner months in advance. That meant that they could keep their phones off on their wedding day and be truly present in the moment.

Plan well, relax and enjoy

Are you keen to enjoy every single moment of your wedding, too? Then make like Mathieu and Vannak and invest in a wedding planner or master of ceremonies to take care of all the details and ensure that your celebration runs smoothly.

Top left Coordinating the menus with the rest
of the stationery makes everything look pulled together.
Top right The traditional Khmer flower garlands bring
good luck, and they look wonderful, too.
Above Accessories from your own country make
the decorations that much more personal.
Right If you are ordering authentic accessories from overseas,
don't forget the delivery times and any customs duties.
Opposite Plants make a wonderful theme and
carry especially positive symbolism.

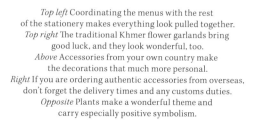

Above Your multicultural wedding requires a change of outfits. This is how you can express your different favorite styles.
Left If you invest in a style-savvy wedding planner like Camille, you can look forward to harmonious arrangements like these.

What to Serve at Your Wedding

From food trucks to wedding cakes: our guide to successful catering

Everyone has to eat! And you can choose from an incredible array of amazing catering options to fit with the style of your celebration. To ensure that all of your guests are catered to, ask about any allergies or intolerances in advance, and provide alternatives for vegetarians and vegans. Little ones will also love child-friendly plates. Bon appétit!

Above At a buffet, your guests will be able to relax and chat with one another, and decide for themselves what, and how much, they want to eat.
Top left After the meal, over coffee, or while you enjoy a cocktail—work out in advance when you want to cut the wedding cake.
Center left Can't decide between a buffet or a sit-down meal? Sharing dishes are a great solution.
Bottom left You'll get perfectly mixed drinks if you invest in a bartender. And your bartender will be able to cater for any special requests your guests may make.

175

Above Enjoy the bar with your eyes, as well. If there are low tables, make sure children and dogs won't upset the carefully wrought arrangements.
Top right Keep enough ice on hand to chill the Champagne, as it won't be great unless its chilled.
Center right Professional wait staff is a worthwhile investment and can make your reception run much more smoothly.
Bottom right Snacks and finger food are always a good idea and provide a great foundation for the welcome drinks before the meal.

Champagne Reception

Raising a glass with your guests after you say "I do" is a lovely custom. "When it comes to the reception, anything goes and nothing is obligatory," says Nessa Buonomo, who runs La Mariée aux Pieds Nus, one of the best French wedding blogs.

"Crémant or Champagne are the classic choices, but you could also serve cocktails, mocktails, juice, or even wine. Whatever you choose, make sure that people are drinking slowly, and serve little canapés too, to tide everyone over until the main meal."

"Make sure to offer alcohol-free options at the welcome drinks, and small, preferably salty, snacks. After a snack, Crémant, Champagne, and gin and tonic don't go to your head so quickly."

Seating Plan

A seating plan might sound old-fashioned, but you'll find that it pays off. It's best to start your planning once everyone has RSVPed, but be prepared to make some last-minute changes. Nessa's advice is to always seat at least two people who already know each other at each table. Group your guests by age or interest, and seat foreign guests at tables where they can converse with others who speak good English. Mixed tables of couples and singles work better than tables full of singles. Teenagers on their own are likely to prefer sitting at tables with young adults, rather than being consigned to the kids' table. Your own table should be where all of the guests can see you. It's customary to have your parents and witnesses sitting with you, but it's not a must. Free software like Tablerrr or Wedding Wire can help you put together your seating plan.

"As a rule of thumb,
put at least two guests who
know each other
at each table, and place single
people at mixed tables."

Above Most venues specify the shape of the table, but offer a variety of table layouts from which you can select for the setup you want.
Top left Place settings look particularly attractive when the guests are given a small decoration next to their name card.
Center left The centerpiece shouldn't be higher than your eyeline, so that your guests can see well and talk across the table.
Bottom left Make sure that all your guests can see you and the speech-makers easily from their seats.

Above What about hiring a food truck? Most providers calculate their prices based on the number of people
multiplied by the price per dish and work to a minimum budget.
Top right Crushed ice dilutes a drink fastest, whereas large ice cubes melt more slowly because of their lower relative surface area.
Center right The table decorations should be stable so that they don't collapse during the toasts!
Bottom right The buffet is itself a decoration with a tasteful mix of snack plates, flowers, and accessories.

180

Drinks

In addition to a good selection of wine, beer, and spirits, make sure you offer non-alcoholic drinks like fruit spritzers or mocktails, and have still and sparkling water in plentiful supply.

If you're planning a big meal, your caterer will be happy to help you choose the wine and work out the quantities. Be mindful of whether your guests will need to drive afterwards! You could also set up a gin bar or offer your own signature cocktails bearing your name.

A Classic Reception

The traditional and most expensive version of the wedding reception is still a sophisticated sit-down meal, served over several courses.

The art here is to plan a meal that everyone will enjoy. Alternatively, a classic buffet will cater to different preferences, while also bringing your guests together as they fill up their plates.

"Each cocktail is only as good as its least good ingredient. Go for quality spirits, mixers, and ice."

Dig in!

What if you're not a fan of all the traditional trappings, but still want to sit down and eat with your guests? Why not place large platters of food in the middle of the tables, along with plates for guests to help themselves? This combines the advantages of a sit-down meal and a buffet. "Go for a pretty arrangement of serving dishes: you could use cake stands, vintage crockery, or big slabs of slate," says Nessa. This is easy to do with the help of family and friends—and it doubles as table decorations, too.

Food Truck

Base your choice of food truck on its style and the cooking that comes out of it, both of which should match your wedding vibe. The food truck team should provide enough servings for all of your guests and dish up the food quickly and professionally. For a larger celebration, having two trucks provides a bigger choice of food and will ensure that lines are shorter. And remember to okay all of this with your wedding venue!

"Food trucks can be a simple way to serve at open-air weddings, and they serve everything from pulled pork and burgers to coffee and cakes. And, as they have their own generators and water tanks, they can be self-sufficient."

Above Keep enough water on hand, as celebrating is thirsty work. And, incidentally, it makes it easier to digest wine and cocktails.
Top left Does your venue come with wait staff? Then get to know the team in advance
so that you feel assured of their friendliness and professionalism.
Center left How wonderful that nature has created so many decorative fruits.
Bottom left The buffet is open. If you have a large number of guests, you could operate a sequence, arranged by table number, for instance.

Above Tasting the cake at the baker's must be one of the best parts of preparing for a wedding.
Top right Dreaming of a cake with a miniature replica of your dream car or with a special finish?
Your baker will be pleased to fulfill any unusual requests.
Center right Not all of your guests will be cake fans, and after a polite taste, some will prefer something lighter.
Bottom right Finger food can be sweet, too. Think about your small guests, too, and offer some children's treats.

Sweet Treats

Coffee and wedding cake traditionally feature at a wedding reception, but sweet tables are also popular, piled with treats to delight guests of all ages. You could also serve dessert buffet-style after the main sit-down meal. This allows everyone to stretch their legs and mingle with guests from other tables.

The Wedding Cake

Weddings just wouldn't be the same without cake! From traditional multi-tiered white confections to unconventional designer cakes, you can go for anything you fancy. "Order your wedding cake at least six months before the big day," advises Nessa.

"Take a few mood board pictures along to your first meeting with the cakemaker—not just of cakes that you like, but also to give an idea of the style of your wedding, the wedding dress, your color scheme, and so on." Choose a cakemaker that specializes in wedding cakes and ask whether you can do a sampling. You may be able to gauge the attention that a cakemaker will devote to your wedding cake by the time that he or she takes to talk to you.

"You can find great
ideas for your wedding cake
on Instagram under
the #weddingcake and
#cakeart hashtags."

Evening Reception

Are you planning an evening wedding without a big evening meal? Then have some delicious canapés, desserts, and cocktails ready for your guests! A good time to start the celebration is around 8 p.m., so that your guests have enough time to have dinner and get dressed beforehand. The midnight snack is a popular tradition: serve something savory like platters of sausages, cheese, or fries. Chili con carne or hot dogs are also bound to garner rave reviews!

Party Favors

Small, ready-packaged edible gifts make perfect favors to show your appreciation for your guests. Lovingly wrapped candies, a regional specialty, an unusual spice mixture, or seasonal delicacies, whether bought or homemade, are a tasteful way of thanking those in attendance for celebrating your big day with you!

"The evening party engine
runs best on fuel in
the form of salty snacks, full-fat
finger food, and
of course, really good drinks.
Serve iced lemon water, too."

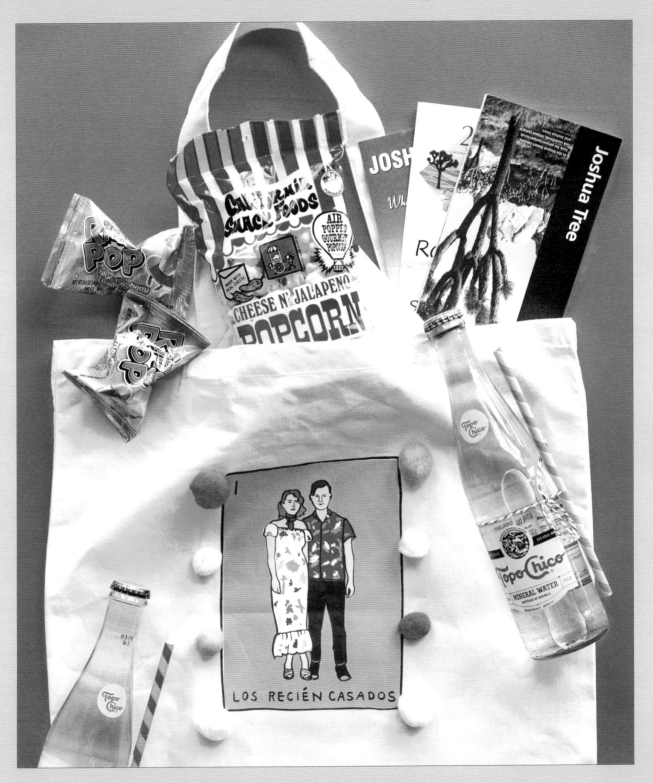

Above See how magical goody bags for your wedding guests can be. Personal details such as this printed bag are especially great.
Top left Discuss gluten-free, kosher, and vegan snacks as alternatives to the usual ones with your caterer.
Center left Every dry cleaner knows that the best finger food doesn't stick or leave a greasy fingermark behind.
Bottom left Napkins and party skewers are a great idea for any party. You could also put a sachet with a wet wipe next to every place setting.

187

A Flower-Bedecked Stoop Wedding

Gaby and Timah hosted a Covid-secure wedding
on the stoop of a historic house in Brooklyn and livestreamed
it for their family and friends

Above With a bit of imagination, even live music can be arranged to be Covid-secure. *Left* Do these magnificent flowers inspire you?
Then take a couple of photos of this wedding and other arrangements with you to your first meeting with your florist.

No sooner had Timah and Gaby moved to Brooklyn together than the Covid-19 pandemic brought New York—and their wedding plans—to a standstill. Just a little while later, however, Timah stumbled upon an Instagram post in which a local florist was raffling off a "stoop wedding" on the steps of a house, complete with gorgeous floral decorations and a Covid-compliant wedding concept. Gaby and Timah put their names into the virtual hat and two weeks later found themselves standing opposite each other on the beautifully decorated Brooklyn stoop, being married by an ordained friend. They were joined by 15 guests live, with another 75 friends and family members watching along on the livestream, not to mention the entire neighborhood cheering the couple on from their balconies!

Join the celebration online

Are you thinking of taking a page out of Timah and Gaby's book and sharing your ceremony online with a few of your loved ones—even in post-Covid times? Then engage the services of a professional videographer or have your best friend livestream the proceedings using a smartphone!

Above Do you know exactly what color flowers you want? Wonderful.
Bottom Agree the color scheme for your celebration with your baker.
Right Then your wedding cake will fit into the big picture perfectly.

Non-Stop Joy Under the Californian Skies

Emily and Calvin held their wedding celebration
in an incredible greenhouse on the Santa Barbara coast, which
combined all the advantages of outdoor and indoor venues

Above If you decorate a glass roof like this one with light strings, the reflections at night are like a sparkling starry sky.
Left The whole effect is so pleasing because the transparent chairs echo the window panes of the greenhouse.

Emily and Calvin's first date and their romantic proposal had both taken place by the sea, so it was only natural for the couple to get married some-where with breathtaking coastal views! They struck gold when they found a natural cliff high above Santa Barbara, and arranged for fairy-tale floral sprays to mark the site of the ceremony on the big day. In a lovely touch, the couple decided to break with tradition and each walk down the aisle with both of their parents. Emily and Calvin chose the enchanting greenhouse on the Dos Pueblos Orchid Farm as the venue for the post-ceremony celebrations. Everyone partied the evening away amid thousands of twinkling lights and a gorgeous color scheme ranging from terracotta to champagne.

Favorite snacks for between times

Are you wondering what sweet treats and quick bites to offer your guests, besides the wedding meal? Emily and Calvin simply served up their favorite snacks, so the five buffet stations were groaning with spicy Cheetos and traditional pies!

Above and bottom Color-coordinated dresses in blush, coral, and rust-red among the bridal party,
while the groom's side looked dapper in matching suspenders.
Right Not all treats have to be fancy! Cheetos and Doritos made a welcome appearance—in keeping with the color palette, no less!

What Better Surprise Than a Big-Top Wedding?

There were plenty of surprises in store for
guests at Katinka and Massimo's dreamy wedding
in Riudecols, Spain, not least a percussion band
and an enormous circus tent

Above If you choose a themed wedding, then do it properly! Use your outfits to pick up the theme and really emphasize it.
Left Why did Katinka and Massimo choose the name "Circus Infinity"? Because of their infinite love.

"If we ever put it up, we'll marry there," promised Massimo, when he and Katinka bought an ancient circus tent a few years ago. Together, they run the wedding venue L'Avellana Mas d'en Cabré, which lies in the green foothills of the Montanyes de Prades some 75 miles from Barcelona. The property is so vast that Katinka and Massimo didn't have much trouble setting up the tent here, much to the delight of their three daughters. It wasn't long before the invitations were in the mail.

Katinka dreamed of a wedding with an opulent, old-time Parisian vibe. She worked with her decorator and florist to adorn the big top with luxurious yet personal details. The long wedding table was resplendent with red and pink floral arrangements. The tent was full of chandeliers heaving with twinkly lights, masses of fresh greenery, golden ornaments, and curios from all over the world. Katinka and Massimo had deliberately not told their guests what to expect—they wanted their new circus to be a surprise!

On the big day, the wedding party gathered for welcome drinks in front of the main house. Suddenly, the Balkan Paradise Orchestra marched around the corner and, with rattling drums and blaring trumpets, led the guests to a big wooden door in the heart of the woods, bearing the inscription "Welcome to the Show" in huge letters. The guests marched through it and were astonished to find the big top, with everything for a major party ready and waiting. Katinka and Massimo made moving vows and exchanged rings, which their daughters brought up to them on pillows that they had woven themselves. Golden confetti fluttered all around them, they kissed, and the party got underway.

Put yourselves center stage

Want to add some personal touches of your own? Then take a leaf out of Katinka and Massimo's book! Bring your wildest dreams to life, use personal items as decoration, and give your very favorite people a role in your ceremony.

Top left You can celebrate as loudly and wildly
as you want at an isolated wedding venue.
Top right The more unusual your wedding cake, the longer
it will live in your and your guests' memories.
Above Whether you choose flower girls or ring bearers, it makes
your heart melt to see children take part in the ceremony.
Right Want to have a spectacular wedding dress
of gold and glitter? Yes, you can.
Opposite Golden detailing, from the chairs to the plate
edges, lends the whole event a real shot of glamour.

Above and left The dramatic red tent, gorgeous flowers, and even
the occasional suspended bicycle added to the whimsical circus theme.
Bottom A dedicated chill-out area for guests to take a breather.

Above Surprise effects and a radiant mood can make your arrival the real highlight for your guests.
Right We are family! If there are quite a few of you already, your favorite little people are automatically on the wedding team.

How to Decorate Your Wedding

Personalize your celebration
with color schemes, lighting,
and accessories

Making your celebration truly magical all comes down to preparation. The more loving consideration, personality, and authenticity that goes into your decorations, the more the magic shines through. "The design sets the mood for the type of celebration you want to have," says Marisa Suarez-Orozco, whose event studio Tropic of Flowers conjures up dreamy moodscapes and exquisite stationery for weddings all over the world. "Flowers, paper, and decor have the power to transform an environment and create a special and unique experience for you and your guests."

Above The more individual your decor, the more distinctive your wedding. (And Jaimee and Adam still have the two stunning piñatas to this very day.)

Top left Natural table decorations are wonderful and cost nothing. Make sure you only cut branches to where you are allowed.

Center left From the pretty invitations to place cards in a matching design, the stationery reinforces the style of your wedding.

Bottom left Complementary colors and materials are held together here by similar vertical patterns.

213

Above Rugs and wall hangings can be used to mark out inviting little seating nooks, providing structure in a low-key manner.
Top right Decorations in matching shades are given a real glamour update with shimmery disco balls like these.
Center right With extraordinary details or accessories you can personalize your wedding celebration.
Bottom right You normally put the flower arrangement on the hood, but it's a nice twist to place it on the trunk of your car instead.

Choose Your Theme

Do you want a chic, modern soiree, a tropical disco dance party, or a romantic dinner under the stars? "I suggest starting by collecting a board of inspiration images," says Marisa. "Consider each of your favorite aesthetics and look around and take inspiration from what you see: your own wardrobe and home decor, for example, or your favorite films and magazines. What styles and color palettes do you naturally gravitate towards as a couple? Modern or classic? Bold or romantic? Start by gathering images you both love, and from there, you can see the themes that emerge. You can then narrow down your wedding vision." The location that you've chosen for your wedding (see p. 36 for tips) provides the framework for the decorative scheme and the style of the invitations. With country or beach weddings, the surroundings often provide enough adornment, so you can get away with just a few accessories. Minimalistic halls are like a blank canvas that allow you to give your creativity free rein, but doing that usually means spending more on decoration. Farmyards, lodges, and rooftops will suggest particular styles that you can either accentuate or contrast with using the right decorative elements.

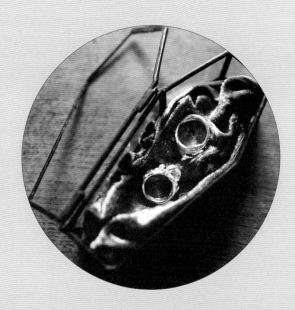

"Consider each of your favorite aesthetics and look around and take inspiration from what you see: your own wardrobe and home decor, for example, or your favorite films and magazines"

The Ceremony

If ever something was worth carefully crafting a beautiful ambience around, it's the moment you say "I do." Will you be holding a summery bohemian wedding in your own backyard? In that case, you could fashion the traditional wedding arch yourself using wooden slats. This works especially well with lots of greenery, gold, vibrant color accents, pampas grass, and fluttering ribbons. Choose comfortable, decorative chairs, benches, or hay bales as seating for your guests, and set up a welcome sign and order of service. If the venue permits, hang garlands or strings of lights overhead along the aisle leading up to the wedding arch or altar. Rugs in complementary colors complete the look.

"Pay full attention to
your wedding arch or the altar
when you're decorating,
as this is the visual centerpiece
of your ceremony."

Above With any luck, you will find a florist who can frame your ceremony with a masterpiece like this.
Top left The bridal bouquet is part of both your outfit and the decor. A good florist will shape it as a visual link between the two.
Center left A colorful garland works like confetti and is bound to create a great atmosphere.
Bottom left You can order build-it-yourself wedding arches on the internet without a problem. You will find a huge range,
from the traditional semi-circular to hexagonal and circular ones.

217

Above Your table decorations will look especially attractive if they pick up the colors and shapes of their surroundings.
Top right Here the red glasses and red flowers successfully echo the red of the big-top roof.
Center right Make sure the table decorations look at their most attractive when you are seated. What do you see first?
And nothing should interrupt the view of the guests opposite.
Bottom right The table cloths and the empty plates are the backdrop to everything else on the table.

218

Dinner is Served!

Will your reception involve a sit-down meal? Set out your favorite crockery alongside flower arrangements, candles, menus, and place cards. Colorful tablecloths are brilliant for adding a splash of color, says Marisa: "We're seeing a shift from traditional whites and blushes in favor of bolder color palettes and décor." You could opt for a botanical theme with little succulents, which also double as pretty guest favors. Wooden elements like coasters, branches, and cutlery handles create a rustic vibe, while lace and floral prints can be used to conjure up a vintage look. If you're celebrating outdoors, lay out picnic blankets and set up a few cocktail tables with pretty centerpieces. You could pair a vase of colorful flowers with a candle holder and a stand with an order of the day card in a suitable design. One design trick is to arrange an odd number of decorative objects at different heights for a pulled-together look—give it a try!

"The table decorations are one of the most important tasks because you will spend a lot of time at the table with your guests."

Let There be Light!

The right lighting is just as important as the music. Having lots of different sources of light gives your venue a balanced, harmonious atmosphere. Candles conjure up a sense of warmth, paper lanterns create a playful effect, lamps look rustic, and fine candlesticks exude sophistication. You could line the dance floor and show the way to the toilets with pin spots and light strings. Consider sourcing your chosen lighting from your local decoration rental outlet—renting lighting can help cut costs. When evening falls, place candles on ledges and windowsills, with mirrors behind them for double the effect. Your wedding photos will also look incredible with warm lighting.

"Candles conjure up a sense of warmth, paper lanterns create a playful effect, lamps look rustic, and fine candlesticks exude sophistication."

Above Indirect light from frosted lamps has a softer effect and is gentler on the eyes than direct light from clear light bulbs.
Top left Light strings arranged in parallel above the scenery give off a uniform light and also create the effect of the night sky.
Left center Well-placed suncatchers cast small points of light across the room and are less obtrusive than large disco balls.
Bottom left Make sure that any open flames, like candles, are placed well out of reach of children and dogs.

221

Above At any relaxed celebration, certain objects will find their way onto the dance floor! If you can, choose decorations that
are robust but it doesn't matter if they break.
Top right Want to really let rip? Then make that clear in your invitation, so that your guests can prepare for the party mentally and when deciding what to wear.
Right center Anything goes! Garlands in all sorts of shapes and colors add a festive feel to any venue.
Bottom right Should your decor carry a message? What about, "On the dance floor, baby!"

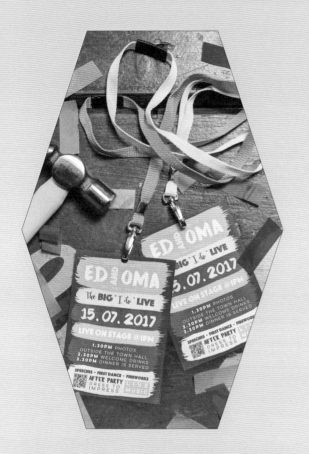

Party Time!

Combine the decorative with the useful! A vintage coffee cart brings a touch of elegance, and it can also be used to serve cappuccinos and Americanos for your guests. Another idea is to rent a pretty carousel to entertain any children at the party; later, it also offers an enchanting backdrop for photos. Besides their entertainment factor, photo booths, hammocks, teepees, and lawn games have the handy side effect of simply looking great. They are also useful for marking out different areas and encouraging your guests to mingle. "Being in lockdown has made people more excited than ever to celebrate," says Marisa. "I believe couples will want to make more of a statement with their wedding designs." You can really go to town when it comes to decorating the dance floor. Rent palm trees and place them around the edges, hang up a giant disco ball, or fill a kiddie pool with inflatable plastic guitars: the only limit is your imagination!

Your decorative scheme is one way of showing off your unique personalities and putting the two of you center-stage as a couple. Let the magic in—and don't be afraid to express yourselves!

"This is the best time
for extravagant party ideas.
After months of
lockdown, your wedding
guests are really in the mood
to party."

Indian Splendor against a Moorish Backdrop

After their ceremony in Seville's most luxurious hotel,
Raisha and Nikhil continued their opulent celebration in
a dreamy 18th-century hacienda

Above Last but not least, your wedding is also something sacred. Throughout the celebration, everything comes back to you and to this special moment.
Left The weather is a matter of chance, but if you look at the weather forecasts for the last few years, perhaps you will be able to find a date which has more than average sunshine!

The city of Seville in southern Spain is so gorgeous that Raisha and Nikhil celebrated their wedding in no fewer than three of its most stunning spots. The Moorish architecture of the Villa Luisa provided the perfect setting for photographing their exquisite wedding outfits; both bride and groom had several changes of ensemble. The luxurious Hotel Alfonso XIII was the venue for the ceremony itself, complete with Hindu traditions like the *Granthi Bandhanam,* in which the bride's saree is tied to the groom's sash. The couple then walked seven steps together, *Saptapadi,* symbolizing

love, prosperity, strength, children, a long life, good food, and happiness. The latter two wishes were granted right away, with dinner and dancing in the courtyard of the 18th-century Hacienda Molinillos.

Moving pictures

Raisha and Nikhil are firmly in the "more is more" camp. To capture the incredible memories from their exuberant wedding, they hired a videographer to edit the highlight moments of their big day into a movie.

Above Traditions can be re-interpreted for today.
Bottom A fortune-teller at your wedding? Great idea.
Right Table decorations about this high leave the view across the table completely free.

VEINTITRES

Above Henna—mehndi, in Hindi—symbolizes love and good fortune.
Bottom In any culture, the arrival of the bride is one of the most important moments at a wedding.
Left Small private spaces provide for moments of contemplation.

A Fiesta of Palms and Piñatas

Jaimee and Adam organized their entire
wedding celebration themselves, from the invitations to the
decorations. The result: a riot of color in the desert

WELCOME

we're so happy you're here!

FRI

SATUR

SUN

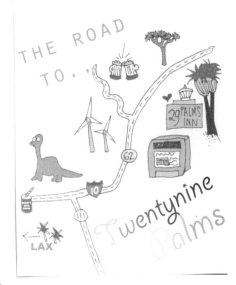

THE ROAD TO...

LAX

Twentynine Palms

2

LA PALMA

6

BEBES DE PIEL

1

LOS RECIÉN CASADOS

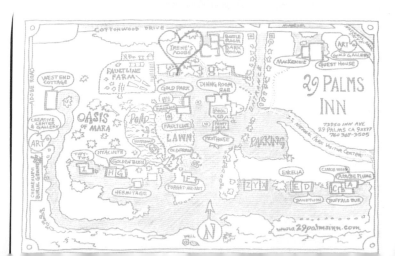

29 PALMS INN

Above The piñatas themselves, which stand in the inside yard of this California desert hotel, are even sweeter than the candy inside them.
Left If you create your whole wedding yourself, from the invitations to the table decorations, then your celebration will bear your own unique signature.

Jaimee and Adam had already been together for 14 years when they decided to make their love official. They tied the knot with only their immediate family in attendance, but when it came to organizing a big party a few months later, they decided on the enchanting 29 Palms Inn on the edge of Joshua Tree National Park, which has a western vibe and glorious views of California's desert skies.

As the owner of a popular vintage store, Jaimee is a consummate organizer and knows how to pull different colors and materials together to create a unique atmosphere. The couple decided not to employ a wedding planner, but to arrange a party for 40 guests themselves. For a Mexican-inspired look, Jaimee and Adam hung piñatas of all shapes and colors around the inner courtyard of the 29 Palms Inn. To these they added colorful strings of flags and bright table decorations made up of floral arrangements, paper cacti, and painted porcelain, all on hand-embroidered tablecloths.

Jaimee and Adam's gorgeous wedding outfits also chimed beautifully with the color scheme. The couple stipulated a bright but monochrome dress code for their guests, and were rewarded with an incredible rainbow effect in their photos. Life-size piñatas of Jaimee and Adam watched over the sumptuously bedecked table, but the couple fell so in love with them that they couldn't bring themselves to wield the stick. As if the heavens had been watching all along, the night glowed with countless shooting stars, like exquisite candies raining from the sky.

DIY wedding

Are you doing all of your own wedding planning, too? Then you'll need to be organized, like Jaimee and Adam! Make clear to-do lists and give generous time margins, plus a little extra budget for any last-minute extravagances—your own piñatas, for instance!

Top left Your own lovingly handmade posters show your guests the way to the celebration.
Top right Balloons don't really mix well with cacti, but these paper globes are a great alternative.
Above Whatever you do, choose a wedding venue you have both fallen in love with.
Right What the wedding ring can do, the jacket can do better! If you can't sew yourself, your tailor will be happy to embroider the date of the wedding.
Opposite Buffets bring movement to a wedding meal.

Above If you ask your guests to keep to the same dress code color palette, every photo will be a hit.
Bottom Even the decor is decked out in bright colors.
Left The color concept works really well against the natural clay wall.

A Surprise Wedding with Disco Dancing

These Sydney guests thought they were attending
a 50th birthday party, but it morphed into a glitzy surprise
wedding—surely the recipe for a spectacular party!

Above With performances like this, you are sure to be named party wedding of the year.
Left Did anyone say "more"? Mirrored surfaces like the sparkling tabletops and disco balls double the effect of the sensational balloon and tinsel decor.

How's this for those who aren't so fond of formal wedding invitations: Just invite your guests to a birthday celebration, then when the party's in full swing, announce that you'll be getting married then and there! Sean and Matt did just that. As everyone was raising their cocktail glasses to toast Sean's 50th birthday, the registrar burst in and declared that the couple would be getting married before the big party got underway.

The crowd broke into cheers of delight and astonishment. The couple, who had met dancing 19 years previously, had an absolute ball. Featuring disco balls, fireworks, and drag performances, the touching ceremony culminated in a glorious finale, with Kylie Minogue's *All The Lovers* playing while gigantic rainbow-colored cannons exploded with glitter behind the newlyweds. Weddings don't get any glitzier than this!

Sometimes more *IS* more

Sean and Matt know that it's all about the entertainment. Investing in incredible decorations, booking thrilling performers, and even getting on stage yourself will make your party unforgettable for you and your guests.

A California Photo Studio Art Party

With the help of their artist friends, Tashina and Huy
created a bright and dazzling fantasy realm for the 125 guests
at their avant-garde dream wedding in Los Angeles

Above Of course, you have to have an avant-garde wedding cake for a creative wedding party like this one.
Left The bridal bouquet shines out like a rainbow-colored explosion and coordinates perfectly with the artistic decor of the wedding venue.

A wedding at your workplace wouldn't be everyone's first choice, but it was the natural solution for Huy and Tashina. Together with a group of artist friends, the photographer and stylist transformed one of their favorite photography studios in Los Angeles into a magical and immersive art experience. Huy fashioned a stunning photo wall out of panels of plexiglass in all the colors of the rainbow. Tashina, meanwhile, designed a light installation and her own wedding dress, which features traditional material from Okinawa, Japan, where her family has its roots. A florist friend decorated the area for the ceremony to create an avant-garde dreamscape.

Once the couple had said their beautiful vows and everyone had eaten dinner, it morphed into a dance floor. The newlyweds partied the night away with their 125 guests amid balloons, confetti, and giant golden leaves.

Local venues

If you'd like to integrate your cultural background into your wedding, you could take a page from Tashina's book: she made her own wedding dress from traditional fabric in Okinawa's regal colors and wore a transparent white dress over it for the ceremony.

Above Request the appropriate dress code in the invitations.
Bottom Then the guests will be a great visual match for your decorated table.
Right "Tasks" such as setting off streamers involve and entertain your guests at the same time.

Index

Index

Index

What a Wedding!

New Wedding Planning, Ideas, and Inspiration

This book was conceived, edited, and designed by gestalten.

Edited by Robert Klanten and Elli Stuhler
Contributing editor: Marianne Julia Strauss

Text by Marianne Julia Strauss

Translation from German to English by Maisie Musgrave with Georgia Smith
in association with First Edition Translations Ltd, Cambridge, UK

Head of Design: Niklas Juli
Cover, design and layout by Stefan Morgner
Layout assistance by Antonia Heckenbach

Photo Editor: Madeline Dudley-Yates

Typefaces: Kepler by Robert Slimbach, Millionaire by Raphaël Verona

Cover photography by Jenn Emerling
Backcover images by Maya Maréchal (top left), Liz Dvorkina (top right), Sylvie Rosokoff (bottom)

Printed by NINO Druck GmbH,
Neustadt an der Weinstraße
Made in Germany

Published by gestalten, Berlin 2021
ISBN 978-3-96704-014-2